THE "ABIDING SABBATH"

AND THE

"LORD'S DAY."

THE

$500 AND $1000 PRIZE ESSAYS.

A REVIEW

BY

ALONZO T. JONES.

TEACH Services, Inc.
PUBLISHING
www.TEACHServices.com • (800) 367-1844

World rights reserved. This book or any portion thereof may not be copied or reproduced in any form or manner whatever, except as provided by law, without the written permission of the publisher, except by a reviewer who may quote brief passages in a review.

The author assumes full responsibility for the accuracy of all facts and quotations as cited in this book. The opinions expressed in this book are the author's personal views and interpretations, and do not necessarily reflect those of the publisher.

This book is provided with the understanding that the publisher is not engaged in giving spiritual, legal, medical, or other professional advice. If authoritative advice is needed, the reader should seek the counsel of a competent professional.

Facsimile Reproduction

As this book played a formative role in the development of Christian thought and the publisher feels that this book, with its candor and depth, still holds significance for the church today. Therefore the publisher has chosen to reproduce this historical classic from an original copy. Frequent variations in the quality of the print are unavoidable due to the condition of the original. Thus the print may look darker or lighter or appear to be missing detail, more in some places than in others.

Copyright © 2010 TEACH Services, Inc.
ISBN-13: 978-1-57258-399-3 (Paperback)
Library of Congress Control Number: 2009937367

THE $500 PRIZE ESSAY.

"THE ABIDING SABBATH."

CHAPTER I.

INSTITUTION OF THE SABBATH.

THE late Hon. Richard Fletcher, of Boston, Mass., by his last will, established in charge of the trustees of Dartmouth College, "a fund from the income of which they were to offer, once in two years, a prize of $500 for the essay best adapted" to counteract "the numerous and powerful influences constantly active in drawing professed Christians into fatal conformity with the world, both in spirit and practice." The fifth time of offering the prize fell in 1883. Accordingly the trustees of the fund and of Dartmouth College selected as the "specific theme" of the desired essay, "The Perpetual Obligation of the Lord's Day," and offered the five-hundred-dollar prize for the best. The committee of award was composed of the following gentlemen: "Prof. William Thompson, D. D., Prof. Llewellyn Pratt, D. D., and Rev. George M. Stone, D. D., all of Hartford, Conn." This committee, "after a careful and thorough examination," awarded the prize to an essay which proved to have been written by the Rev. George Elliott, of West Union, Iowa. The essay, entitled "The Abiding Sabbath," appeared in 1884, and was issued from the press of the American Tract Society in the winter of 1884-85, in the form of a book of two hundred and eighty pages.

There is no use in disputing the fact that the Sunday question is fast becoming the leading question of the day. Large conventions of ministers are held solely to secure its enforced observance by the civil power; the W. C. T. U. works it up all over the United States; Prohibition Conventions put it in their platforms; Legislatures, both State and National, from beginning to end of their sessions are petitioned for the enactment of stringent laws in its behalf; the religious papers of the country lift up one united cry that it must and shall be preserved; political conventions are "worked" and Legislatures are "lobbied" in the interests of the Sunday; Knights of Labor, workingmen's unions, and Socialists call loudly for laws enforcing its observance; and colleges and religious publication societies offer large prize essays for arguments to sustain it. All these things are significant and worthy of attention. "The Abiding Sabbath" being one of the latest as well as one of the most authoritative discussions of the question as to why Sunday should be kept, we ask the attention of the reader while we examine the main points of the argument.

The book is divided into three parts,—"Sabbath of Nature," "Sabbath of the Law," and "Sabbath of Redemption." We shall quote quite largely from the first two parts, and that without argument, there being in fact no room for argument between us, because the author of "The Abiding Sabbath," in these two parts, proves to perfection the perpetual obligation of the seventh day as the Sabbath, and that is exactly what we believe. We ask our readers to study carefully his argument on the "Sabbath of Nature" and the "Sabbath of the Law," which we quote, (1) because it is excellent reading, and (2) because we want them to see clearly, by what curious freaks of logic it is, that after absolutely demonstrating the perpetual obligation of the seventh day, another day entirely is to be observed. He says most truly:—

"The Sabbath is an institution as old as the completion of the world. . . . It shares with marriage the glory of being the sole relics saved to the fallen race from their lost paradise. One is the foundation of the family, and consequently of the State; the other is equally necessary to worship and the church. These two fair and fragrant roses man bore with him from the blighted bliss of Eden.

"It is not, however, the mere fact of age that lends sacredness to these institutions; for years alone cannot give consecration or compel regard to anything which does not possess in itself some inherent sanctity and dignity. It is in the circumstances of its first institution, and in its essential character, that we must hope to discover the necessity and holiness of the Sabbath day.

"'God blessed the seventh day and sanctified it, because that in it he had rested from all his work which God created and made.' Gen. 2 : 3. Such is the sublimely simple statement which forms the last strain of that magnificent hymn of creation which is our only glimpse into the beginning of things. It is surely consistent with sound common sense and sound interpretation to see in these words much more than a mere anticipation of the theocratic Sabbath of Israel. It seems absurd to express in words what some have implied in their reasonings on this passage: 'God rested on the seventh day; therefore 2,500 years afterwards he blessed and sanctified it.' The same form of language is used to describe what took place on the seventh day as in relating what took place in the six preceding days.

"It is certain that a first reading of this passage conveys to the mind the idea that the sanctification of the Sabbath as a day of rest took place at the very close of the creative week. That such was the case would probably never have been denied, if the denial had not been necessary to support a peculiar view. Doubt in regard to this proleptic interpretation is sustained by the recent discovery of mention of a day of rest in the Assyrian account of creation, which is believed to antedate Moses by nearly six hundred years, and the further discovery of the actual observance of a Sabbath in Babylonia long before the time of the Mosaic institution. Is not God saving his facts, in Egyptian tombs, on Assyrian bricks, and in all historic remains everywhere, that, at every crisis of his truth, when even the mouths of believers are silenced by the tumult of doubt, the very 'stones' may 'cry out'? . . .

"A special authority attaches itself to the primitive revelation. Whatever critical opinions may assert concerning the early history of the world, to the Christian the testimony of Jesus Christ remains in force to the high obligation of the Edenic law. In reproving the corruptions of the marriage relation which had arisen under the Mosaic code, he reverts to the primitive law: 'From the beginning it was not so.' That is to say, the law of the beginning is supreme. Whatever institutions were given to man then were given for all time. There is given thus to marriage, and to its related institution, the Sabbath, a permanent character and authority which transcend the Hebrew legislation in their universal and binding force. Those elements of truth which were given to the infant race, are the possession of humanity, and not of the Jew alone; they are the alphabet of all the growing knowledge of man, not to be forgotten as the world grows old, but to be borne with him in all his wanderings, to last through all changes, and be his guide up those rugged steeps by which he must climb to the lofty summits of his nobler destiny.

"Not to a single race, but to man; not to man alone, but to the whole creation; not to the created things alone, but to the Creator himself, came the benediction of the first Sabbath. Its significance extends beyond the narrow limits of Judaism, to all races, and perhaps to all worlds. It is a law spoken not simply through the lawgiver of a chosen people, but declared in the presence of a finished heaven and earth. The declaration in Genesis furnishes the best commentary on the saying of Jesus: 'The Sabbath was made for man.' For man, universal humanity, it was given with its benediction.

"The reason of the institution of the Sabbath is one which possesses an unchanging interest and importance to all mankind. The theme of the creation is not peculiar to Israel, nor is worship of the Creator confined to the children of Abraham. The primary article of every religious creed, and the foundation of all true religion, is faith in one God as the Maker of all things. Against atheism, which denies the existence of a personal God; against materialism, which denies that this visible universe has its roots in the unseen; and against secularism, which denies the need of worship, the Sabbath is therefore an eternal witness. It symbolically commemorates that creative power which spoke all things into being, the wisdom which ordered their adaptations and harmony, and the love which made, as well as pronounced, all 'very good.' It is set as the perpetual guardian of man against that spiritual infirmity which has everywhere led him to a denial of the God who made him, or to the degradation of that God into a creature made with his own hands."

Further he says:—

"While the reason remains, the law remains. The reason of the Sabbath is to be found in the fact of creation; it is God's one monument set in human history to that great event; and so long as the truth of creation and the knowledge of a Creator have any value to human thought, any authority over the human conscience, or make any appeal to human affections, so long the law and the institution of the Sabbath will abide with lasting instruction and undiminished obligation.

"God 'rested the seventh day from all his work which he had made.' Such is the record, declared in the beginning, embodied in the decalogue, and confirmed by the epistle to the Hebrews. It is a statement not to be easily understood at the first glance 'Hast thou not known? hast thou not heard, that the everlasting God, the Lord, the Creator of the ends of the earth, fainteth not, neither is weary?' Isa. 40:28. If he is never weary how can we say of him that he rests? . . . God is a Spirit, and the only rest which he can know is that supreme repose which only the Spirit can know—in the fulfillment of his purpose and the completeness as well as completion of his work. Just as, in the solemn pauses between the creative days, he pronounced his creatures 'very good,' so did he rejoice over the finishing of his work, resting in the perfect satisfaction of an accomplished plan; not to restore his wasted energy, as man rests, but to signify that in the coming of man the creative idea has found its consummation and crown. Such is the rest possible to a purely spiritual nature—the rest of a completed work. . . .

"There is a still deeper sense in which the example of Deity reveals this obligation. Suppose the question to be asked, How can we know that any precept is moral in its meaning and authority, and not simply a positive and arbitrary command? What better answer could be given to this inquiry than to say that a moral precept must have the ground of its existence in the nature of God? Our highest conception of the moral law is to regard it as the transcript of his nature. . . . No more perfect vindication of the moral character of a law can be given than to show that it is a rule of the divine conduct; that it has been imposed upon his own activity by that infinite Will which is the supreme authority both in the physical and moral government of the universe. That law to which the Creator submits his own being must be of absolute binding force upon every creature made in his image. Such is the law of the Sabbath. 'God rested the seventh day,' and by so doing has given to the law of the Sabbath the highest and strongest sanction possible even to Deity. In no conceivable way could the Almighty so perfectly and with such unchallengeable authority declare, not simply his will in a positive institution, but the essentially moral character of the precept, as by revealing his own self-subjection to the rule which he imposes on his creatures. . . .
Its obligation is addressed, not to man's physical

nature alone, but to man as a spiritual being, made in the image of God; it is laid, not only on his bodily powers and natural understanding, but upon his moral reason as right, and upon his conscience as duty. It is therefore bounded by no limits of time, place, or circumstance, but is of universal and perpetual authority."

Then he closes Chapter I of his book with the following most just conclusion:—

"The Sabbath is therefore shown to be given in the beginning to all men; to have the lofty sanction of the example of God; to be rooted in the eternal world; to be the witness of the most important truths possible for man to know; to be a blessing to man's nature; to inclose a duty of worship to God. By all these revealings which are given by the institution at its first ordainment, we are justified in believing that it has a moral meaning within it, and imposes upon all races and generations of men an unchanging and unrelaxed obligation of dutiful observance."

We have quoted more than half of the whole first chapter; but we have no apology to make. We honestly thank Mr. Elliott that he has given us so masterly a demonstration of the perpetual and universal obligation of the seventh day as the Sabbath of the Lord. Again we ask the reader to study it carefully; for it is a vindication of principles that are eternal, and that no ingenuity of man can undermine.

CHAPTER II.

SABBATH OF THE LAW.

As a basis for the further notice of "The Abiding Sabbath," we shall here give some extracts from the author's discussion of the fourth commandment, showing the universal and everlasting obligation of the seventh day as the Sabbath of the Lord. He says:—

"The giving of the law at Sinai is the loftiest landmark in the history of Israel. It is the beginning of their civil and religious polity. From that moment Israel became the nation of Jehovah, the nation of the law, the leader among the nations of the earth in the search after a positive righteousness. That the Sabbath is a part of that code, has therefore a meaning not for the Hebrew alone, but for the whole race of mankind.

"Everywhere in the sacred writings of the Hebrews they are reminded that they are the people peculiarly guided by Providence. Historian, psalmist, and prophet never tire in recounting the marvelous interpositions of Jehovah in behalf of his chosen people. And this thought is the key-note to the decalogue, 'I am the Lord thy God, which have brought thee out of the land of Egypt, out of the house of bondage'

(Ex. 20:2), is the introduction to the law. When therefore the Sabbath is introduced into the decalogue, while its old significance as a testimony of creation is not lost, but especially recalled, it becomes, beside, a monument of the divine Providence whose particular manifestations Israel, among the nations, has most largely experienced. The Sabbath of the law is the Sabbath of Providence.

"The declaration on Sinai is perhaps the strongest attestation which the Sabbatic ordinance has received. It is henceforth based upon an express command of God himself, is given in circumstances of the most impressive solemnity, and has received the awful sanction of embodiment in the moral law, against which 'the soul that sinneth, it shall die.' Eze. 18:4. God has spoken, and his creatures must obey or perish.

"We commonly speak of the decalogue as the 'ten commandments.' A more precise rendering of the Hebrew terms would be the 'ten words' (Ex. 34:28, margin; Deut. 4:13; 10:2, 4, margin), an exact equivalent of which we have taken from the Greek, in the word 'decalogue.' These statutes are therefore not simply commands or precepts of God, for God may give commandments which have only a transient and local effect; they are in a distinctive sense the word of God, an essential part of that word which 'abideth.' In the decalogue we get a glimpse of that inner movement of the divine will which is the permanent foundation for all temporary ordinances. It is not contended that this language is rigidly uniform, but only that by the phrase, 'the ten words,' as well as in the general scope of Hebrew legislation, the moral law is fully distinguished from the civil and ceremonial law. The first is an abiding statement of the divine will; the last consists of transient ordinances having but a temporary and local meaning and force. The decalogue is also called the 'testimony' (Ex. 25: 16 and in many other places), that is, the witness of the divine will; also the words of the 'covenant' (34: 28), and 'his (*i. e.*, Jehovah's) covenant' (Deut. 4: 13), upon obedience to which his favor was in a special manner conditioned. The names given to this code declare its unchanging moral authority.

"The manner in which this law was given attests its special sanctity and high authority. Before its announcement, the people of Israel, by solemn rites, sanctified themselves, while the holy mountain was girded with the death-line which no mortal could pass and live. When the appointed day came, to the sublime accompaniment of pealing thunders and flashing lightnings, the loud shrilling of angel-blown trumpets, the smoking mountain, and the quaking earth, from the lips of Jehovah himself sounded forth 'with a great voice' the awful sentences of this divine law, to which in the same way 'he added no more.' Deut. 5:22. Not by the mouth of an angel or prophet came this sublimest code of morals, but the words were formed in air by the power of the Eternal himself. And when it was to be recorded, no human scribe took down the sacred utterances; they were engraved by no angel hand; but with his own finger he inscribed on tables of stone, whose preparation, in the first instance, was 'the work of God,' the words of his will. Ex. 31:18; 32:16; 34:1, 4, 28.

"The law declared by his own mouth and indited by his own hand was finally placed in the ark of the covenant, underneath the mercy-seat, where sprinkled blood might atone for its violation; . . and beneath the flaming manifestation of the very presence of the Almighty, the glory of the shekinah; circumstances signifying forever the divine source of this law and the divine solicitude that it should be obeyed. This superior solemnity and majesty of announcement and conservation distinguish the decalogue above all other laws given to man, and separate it widely from the civil polity and ritual afterwards given by the hand of Moses. These latter are written by no almighty finger and spoken to the people by no divine voice; for these it is sufficient that Moses hear and record them.

"Of the law thus impressively given, the fourth commandment forms a part. Amid the same cloud of glory, the same thunders and lightnings, uttered by the same dread voice of the Infinite One, and graven by his finger, came forth these words as well: 'Remember the Sabbath day to keep it holy.' It is impossible, in view of these facts, to class the Sabbath with the ceremonial institutions of Israel. By the sacred seal of the divine lip and finger, it has been raised far above those perishing rites. In other words, it belongs to that moral law which Paul calls 'holy, and just, and good' (Rom. 7:12), and not that ritual law of which Peter declares, 'Neither our fathers nor we were able to bear' it. Acts. 15:10.

"Nothing can be found in the form of words in which the fourth commandment is expressed which indicates that it is less universal in its obligation or less absolute in its authority than the other nine with which it is associated. . . . But it is sometimes claimed that this is simply a Mosaic institute, and therefore of transient force; that this has not, like the others, an inward reason which appeals to the conscience; that it is, in short, not a moral but a positive precept. ? .

"The proof which would exclude this commandment from the throne of moral authority on which the others are seated should amount to demonstration. . . . The distinction cannot be maintained between this commandment and the remainder of the decalogue. The prohibition of image-worship is not deemed essential by either Roman or Greek Christianity; but the more spiritual mind of Protestantism can see that this law is absolutely necessary to guard a truly spiritual conception of Deity. So, many excellent Christians have failed to discern the moral necessity of the Sabbath. Clearer insight will reveal that all the laws of the first table are guarded by this institution, as all in the second table are enforced by the tenth, 'Thou shalt not covet.' . . .

"The moral authority of the decalogue did not begin with its announcement on Sinai. Its precepts had been known and practised through all the patriarchal ages. Murder was condemned in Cain, and dishonor of parents in Ham. To Abraham, Isaac, and Jacob had come the knowledge of one God, and the last had exhorted his children against image-worship. Gen. 35:2. Theft, falsehood, and adultery are all denounced by the record of pre-Mosaic times. As a declaration of the eternal and unchanging moral law its binding force did not begin with its announcement at Horeb, but dated from the beginning of things, and for the same reason will endure until the consummation of all things. Nor was it given to Israel alone. The Gentiles 'show the work of the law written in their hearts.' Rom. 2:14, 15.

"Jesus Christ has confirmed its obligation: 'If thou wilt enter into life, keep the commandments.' Matt. 19:17. His great generalization of the whole law, into the double duty of love to God and man is a further confirmation of the persistence of its ethical force. James writes: 'Whosoever shall keep the whole law, and yet offend in one point, he is guilty of all. For he that said, Do not commit adultery, said also, Do not kill. Now if thou commit no adultery, yet if thou kill, thou art become a transgressor of the law.' James 2: 10, 11. It is impossible to suppose that the apostle has not in mind the whole decalogue, and that he does not equally affirm the profaner of the Sabbath to be a violator of the whole law. In a statement of such gravity he must have specified the exception if any existed. It is worthy of our notice that he bases the sanctity of each command on the fact that each was spoken by one God. But the law of the Sabbath was as surely uttered by the voice of Jehovah as any other precept of the ten. If the 'ten words' of Sinai live to-day, imposing an unrelaxed obligation upon all mankind, as is testified both by the nature of the legislation and by the authority of Jesus and his apostles, the Sabbath shares their perpetuity, both of existence and obligation. . . .

"In the law spoken by the mouth of God himself and written by his own finger, the transcript of his will, the reasons assigned for the institution of the Sabbath are such as appeal, not to Israel alone, but to man as man. The Sabbath recalls a fact of universal interest, the creation of the world, and is based on a process in the nature of God, who in some ineffable way 'rested on the seventh day.' The ideas connected with the Sabbath in the fourth commandment are thus of the most permanent and universal meaning. The institution, in the light of the reasons assigned, is as wide as the creation and as eternal as the Creator.

"Instituted at the creation by the example of the Creator, its obligation extends to every creature. It is inconceivable, on any theory of inspiration, that any narrower interpretation is to be given to this command. If language is to have any meaning at all, the Sabbath of the fourth commandment is not simply an Israelitish, but a human institution. As it answers a universal need, so is it enforced by a universal reason, being supported by the only state of facts that could create a perpetual institute,—the law of the beginning. . . .

"These considerations cannot be treated with too much gravity. Long should pause the erring hand of man before it dares to chip away with the chisel of human reasonings one single word graven on the enduring tables by the hand of the infinite God. What is proposed? To make an erasure in a Heaven-born code; to expunge one article from the recorded will of the Eternal! Is the eternal tablet of his law to be defaced by a creature's hand? He who proposes such an act should fortify himself by reasons as holy as God and as mighty as his power. None but consecrated hands could touch the ark of God; thrice holy should be the hands which would dare alter the testimony which lay within the ark.

"By the lasting authority of the whole decalogue, with which the fourth commandment is inseparably connected, which is the embodiment of immutable moral law, and *by the very words used in framing the command*, the Sabbath is shown to be an institution of absolute, universal, and unchanging obligation.

"Here may properly be inserted that prayer which the Anglican Church prescribes as a response to the recitation of each of the ten commandments: 'Lord, have mercy upon us, and incline our hearts to keep this law.'"

Amen! and, Amen! say we.

CHAPTER III.

SOME FIVE-HUNDRED-DOLLAR LOGIC.

It must be borne in mind that the book entitled "The Abiding Sabbath" was written to prove "the perpetual obligation of the Lord's day;" and that by the term "Lord's day," the author of the book means, in every instance, the first day of the week. Therefore, "being interpreted," the book, "The Abiding Sabbath," is an argument to prove the perpetual obligation of the first day of the week. It is likewise to be remembered that the trustees of Dartmouth College paid the Fletcher prize of five hundred dollars for the essay which composes the book "The Abiding Sabbath." This certainly is tangible proof that those trustees, and the Committee of Award appointed by them, considered that the object of the essay had been accomplished, and that thereby the perpetual obligation of the first day of the week had been proved. But we are certain that any one who has read the two preceding chapters on this subject, will wonder how, in view of the arguments there used, the author can make it appear that the first day of the week is "the abiding Sabbath." Well, to tell in a few words what we shall abundantly demonstrate, he does it by directly contradicting every sound argument that he has made, and every principle that he has established.

In the first chapter of the book, from the scripture "God blessed the seventh day and sanctified it, because that in it he had rested from all his work which God created and made" (Gen. 2: 3), he proves the institution of the Sabbath at creation, and says: "Whatever institutions were given to man then, were given for all time."

And again: "'God rested the seventh day,' and by so doing has given to the law of the Sabbath the highest and strongest sanction possible, even to Deity. . . . It is therefore bounded by no limits of time, place, or circumstance, but is of universal and perpetual authority."

It was the seventh day upon which God rested from the work of creation; it was the seventh day which he then blessed; it was the seventh day which he then sanctified; and he says, "The seventh day is the Sabbath." Now if, as Mr. Elliott says, this institution was given to man "for all time," and that, too, "with the highest and strongest sanction possible even to Deity;" and if it is bounded "by no limits of time, place, or circumstance," how can it be possible that the first day of the week is the abiding Sabbath? It is clearly and absolutely impossible. The two things cannot stand together. God did not rest the first day of the week. He did not bless, nor did he sanctify, the first day of the week. He has never called the first day of the week the Sabbath; nor as such an institution has he ever given it any sanction of Deity, much less has he ever given it the "highest and strongest sanction possible even to Deity." Then upon no principle of truth can it ever be made to appear that the first day of the week is the abiding Sabbath.

Then in Part II, on the fourth commandment,— the "Sabbath of the Law,"—he says of the Sabbath therein given to Israel when God brought them out of Egypt: "The first institution of religion given to the emancipated nation *was the very same* with the *first given to man*" (p. 110). He says that it has "a meaning not for the Hebrews alone, but for the whole race of mankind;" that "the reason of the commandment recalls the ordinance of creation;" that "the ideas connected with the Sabbath in the fourth commandment are thus of the *most permanent* and universal meaning;" and that "the institution, in the light of the reasons assigned, is *as wide as creation and as eternal as the Creator*" (pp. 114, 126).

And yet into this commandment, which says as plainly as language can speak, "The seventh day is the Sabbath of the Lord thy God," Mr. Elliott proposes to read the first day as "the abiding Sabbath."

Before noticing his reasons for such a step, we would repeat one of his own paragraphs:—

"Long should pause the erring hand of man before it dares to chip away with the chisel of human reasonings *one single word* graven on the enduring tables by the hand of the infinite God. What is proposed?

To make an erasure in a Heaven-born code; to expunge one article from the recorded will of the Eternal! Is the eternal tablet of his law to be defaced by a creature's hand? He who proposes such an act *should fortify himself by reasons as holy as God and as mighty as his power.* None but consecrated hands could touch the ark of God; thrice holy should be the hands which would dare to alter the testimony which lay within the ark."—*Pp. 128, 129.*

And so say we.

After proving that the ten commandments are of universal and perpetual obligation, he discovers that the decalogue "contains transient elements." He says:—

"It may be freely admitted that the decalogue in the form in which it is stated, contains transient elements. These, however, are easily separable. For example, the promise attached to the requirement of filial reverence, 'that thy days may be long upon the land which the Lord thy God giveth thee,' has a very evident reference to Israel alone, and is a promise of national perpetuity in possession of the promised land."

But lo, just here he discovers that this is *not* a "transient element," and that it has *not* "reference to Israel alone;" for he continues in the very same paragraph:—

"Even this element is not entirely of limited application, however, for Paul quotes the commandment in his letter to the Christians of Ephesus (Eph. 6: 2), as 'the first . . . with promise,' evidently understanding the covenant of long life to have a wider scope than simply the Hebrew nationality.

And it is clear that nothing can be imagined which could give more enduring stability to civil institutions than that law-abiding character which is based on respect for superiors and obedience to their commands."—*Pp. 120, 121.*

His proposition is that "the decalogue contains transient elements." And to demonstrate his proposition, he produces as an "example," a "transient element" which he immediately proves is not a transient element at all. Then what becomes of his proposition? Well, by every principle of common logic, it is a miserable failure. But by this new, high-priced kind, this five-hundred-dollar-prize logic, it is a brilliant success; for by it he accomplishes all that he intended when he started out; that is, that by it he might put aside as a "transient element" the *seventh day*, and swing into its place the seventh part of time. For after proving that his example of a transient element is not a transient element at all, he continues:—

"This serves to illustrate how we may regard the temporal element in the law of the Sabbath. It does not bind us to the precise day, but to the seventh of our time."

To the trustees of Dartmouth College, and to the Committee of Award which they appointed, and to the American Tract Society, it may serve to illustrate such a thing; but to anybody who loves truth, sound reasoning, and fair dealing, it only serves to illustrate the deplorable weakness of the cause in behalf of which resort has to be made to such subterfuges.

Besides this, his admission that the decalogue contains transient elements is directly contrary to the argument that he has already made on this very subject. On page 116, he had already written of the ten commandments:—

"These statutes are therefore not simply commands or precepts of God; for God may give commandments which have only a transient and local effect; they are *in a distinctive sense* the word of God, an essential part of that word *which 'abideth.'* . . . By the phrase 'the ten words,' as well as in the general scope of Hebrew legislation, the moral law *is fully distinguished* from the civil and ceremonial law. *The first is an abiding statement* of the *divine will; the last consists of transient ordinances* having but a temporary and local meaning."

Yet directly in the face of this, he will have it freely admitted that the decalogue "contains transient elements." Are there transient elements in the divine will? Can that which abideth be transient? And if the decalogue contains transient elements, then wherein is it "fully distinguished" from the "civil and ceremonial law," which "consists of transient ordinances"? The genuine logic of his position is (1) the ceremonial law consists of transient ordinances; (2) the decalogue is fully distinguished from the ceremonial law; (3) therefore the decalogue consists of nothing transient. But with the aid of this five-hundred-dollar-prize logic it is thus: The ceremonial law consists of transient ordinances. The decalogue is fully distinguished from the ceremonial law. Therefore it may be freely admitted that the decalogue contains transient elements!! And so "with the ceremonial system vanished the Jewish Sabbath," which he defines to be the seventh day (pp. 177, 190). By one argument on these transient elements, he manages to put away the precise seventh day, and to put in its place "the seventh of our time;" by another he is enabled to abolish the seventh of our time, as well as the precise seventh day, by which he opens the way to insert in the commandment the precise first day as the "abiding Sabbath" and of "perpetual obligation."

Again we read:—

"While the Sabbath of Israel had features which enforce and illustrate the abiding Sabbath, it must not be forgotten that it had a wholly distinct existence of its own. . . Moses really instituted something new, something different from the old patriarchal seventh day."—*P. 134.*

With this read the following:—

"The first institution of religion given to the emancipated nation was the very same with the first given to man."—*P. 110.*

How the Sabbath of Israel could be the *very same* with the first given to man, and yet have a *wholly distinct existence* of its own; how it could be the "*very* same" with the first given to man, and yet be "something new" 2500 years afterward; how it could be something different from the old patriarchal seventh day, and yet in it there be "still embodied the true Sabbath," we cannot possibly conceive; but perhaps the genius that can discern in the decalogue transient elements which it proves are not transient at all, could also tell how all these things can be.

Just one more illustration of the wonderful feats that can be performed by a prize essay. On page 135 he says:—

"In the Mosaic Sabbath, for the time of its endurance and no longer, was embodied, for a particular people and no others, this permanent institution which was ordained at creation, and which lives now with more excellent glory in the Lord's day."

That is to say: (1) In the Mosaic institution, "for the time of its endurance [1522 years] and no longer," was embodied an institution which is "rooted in the eternal world" (p. 28), and which is as eternal as the Creator (p. 126); (2) in the Mosaic institution, which was "for a particular people and no others," was embodied an institution whose "unrelaxed obligation" extends to "every creature," "to all races of earth and all ages of the world's history" (pp. 122, 124).

In other words, in an institution that was for a particular people and *no others*, for 1522 years and *no longer*, was embodied an institution that is eternal, and for all races in all ages of the world's history.

Now we wish that Mr. Elliott, or some of those who were concerned in paying the five-hundred-dollar prize for this essay, would tell us how it were possible that an institution that is as eternal as the Creator could be embodied in one that was to endure for 1522 years and *no longer;* and how an institution that is of unrelaxed obligation upon all races in all ages, could be embodied in one that was for a particular people and *no others*. And when he has told us that, then we wish he would condescend to inform us how in the Mosaic Sabbath there could be embodied three such diverse elements as (1) the "permanent institution which was ordained at creation," which was the seventh day; (2) "something new," which he says was "not improbably a different day;" and (3) "the institution which lives now with more excellent glory in the Lord's day," which he says is the first day of the week.

We have not the most distant idea, however, that Mr. Elliott, or any one else, will ever explain any of these things. They cannot be explained. They are absolute contradictions throughout. But by them he has paved the way by which he intends to bring in the first day of the week as the abiding Sabbath, and they are a masterly illustration of the methods by which that institution is made to stand.

CHAPTER IV.

"THE SABBATH OF REDEMPTION."

"The Sabbath of Redemption" composes Part III of "The Abiding Sabbath," and in it throughout the author still diligently pursues his course of systematic self-contradiction. The first division of this part is "The Testimony of Jesus Christ" upon the subject of the Sabbath, a few sentences of which we quote. He says:—

"As already shown, the Sabbath contained moral elements; it belonged not solely to Israel, but was sanctioned by the primitive revelation to the race, being the first article in the law of the beginning; it was a part of that sublime code which by the mouth of the Eternal himself was spoken to his chosen people from the mountain of God; its violation had been surrounded, in the Mosaic legislation and in the prophetic instructions, with penalties, and its observance with blessings, such as could hardly be attached to a simple institution of ritual. The abiding Sabbath, belonging to the moral law *is* therefore *not repealed or canceled by Jesus*, but rather confirmed with new uses, loftier meanings, and holier objects."—*P. 159.*

Then in speaking of the "false strictness" with which the Jews had surrounded and obscured the real intent of the Sabbath, and how Jesus swept this all away, he says:—

"There is not in all this any hint of the abolition of the Sabbath, or release from its obligations. The words of Jesus become meaningless when they are applied to anything but the abuses and perversions of its purposes by the Rabbinical schools. Had he desired to abolish it altogether, nothing would have been easier than to do so in terms. His words are everywhere framed with the utmost care, and strictly guarded against any construction which would involve a denial of the real sacredness of the day blessed by the Creator and sanctioned by the moral law."—*P. 163.*

Now the day blessed by the Creator is the seventh day; for "God blessed *the seventh day*" is the word of God, and "*The seventh day* is the Sabbath" is the declaration of God in the moral law. Therefore we submit that as Christ's words are "strictly guarded against any construction which would involve a denial of the real sacredness of the day blessed by the Creator and sanctioned by the moral law," then the word of Christ binds every man to the observance of the seventh day, and forever debars any application of his teaching to any other than the seventh day; for God never blessed any but the seventh day, and none other than the seventh day is sanctified, as the Sabbath, by the moral law.

Again he says:—

"Jesus confirms the Sabbath on its spiritual basis. 'The Sabbath was made for man, and not man for the Sabbath; therefore the Son of man is Lord also of the Sabbath.' . . . Thus he at once rid it of all the false restrictions of Judaism, and, establishing it upon its primitive foundations, he brought forth its higher reason in the assertion of its relation to the well-being of man. 'The Sabbath was made for man;' not for the Jew only, but for the whole race of mankind; not for one age alone, but for man universally, under every circumstance of time and place."—*P. 165*.

Then in another place Mr. Elliott says further:—

"The declaration in Genesis furnishes the best commentary on the saying of Jesus: 'The Sabbath was made for man.'"—*P. 17*.

The "declaration in Genesis" is: "And on the seventh day God ended his work which he had made; and he rested on the seventh day from all his work which he had made. And God blessed the seventh day, and sanctified it; because that in it he had rested from all his work which God created and made." We agree perfectly with Mr. Elliott that that "furnishes the best commentary on the saying of Jesus," in Mark 2:27. It is the Lord's own commentary on his own word; it is his own explanation of his own statement. Therefore when, by any statement in any way, Mr. Elliott or any one else attempts to bring the first day of the week into place as the Sabbath, it is simply doing violence to the word of God, and is in direct contradiction to the divine commentary.

Now in accordance with his scheme throughout, after having, by every principle of logic, established the obligation of the seventh day as the Sabbath, he proceeds at once to contradict it all. He says:—

"'The Son of man is Lord also of the Sabbath.' This is an assertion by our Lord of his right to make such modifications in the law of the Sabbath, and give it such new adjustments as should to him seem best for the religious culture of the race. As Lord of the Sabbath, he doubtless had the power to set it entirely aside,—a power which certainly he has nowhere exercised, either by himself or through his apostles. *He had the right to change its day* and alter or add to its meanings,—a right *which he has exercised* in giving us the Lord's day, the Christian Sabbath, and in making it a monument of redemption as well as of creation and providence. Because he is 'Lord of the Sabbath,' we can rightly call the Sabbath the Lord's day, and the Lord's day our Sabbath. That which he has asserted that he had the power to do, *we have the right to assume he has done,* and we have, moreover, the right to infer that the change which came over the Sabbatic institutions in the early Christian centuries was not without his will, but by his authority and in fulfillment of his purpose."—*Pp. 168, 169.*

Again :—

"More subtly than Moses, yet as really as the lawgiver in the wilderness, he was instituting a new Sabbath."—*P. 172.*

Here are several points, upon each of which we wish to dwell for a moment. We take the last one first: "More subtly than Moses, yet as really he was instituting a new Sabbath." How subtly did Moses institute a new Sabbath? Why not at all, subtly or otherwise. Moses instituted no weekly Sabbath, either new or old. God spoke the word from Heaven: "The seventh day is the Sabbath of the Lord thy God; in it thou shalt not do any work;" as Mr. Elliott himself says, "Not by the mouth of angel or prophet came this sublimest code of morals: but the words were formed in air *by the power of the Eternal himself*" (p. 117). But go back even beyond Sinai, to the Wilderness of Sin, at the falling of the manna, nor yet there was it left to Moses to mark the day that was the Sabbath, much less was it given to him to institute the Sabbath. Here, again, Mr. Elliott states the case precisely: "*God himself* provided the feast in the wilderness which marked for them the weekly recurrence of the holy day. . . . The connection of the miraculous supply of food with the seventh day was certainly calculated to strongly impress the Sabbath upon the thoughts and imaginations of the people, and thus was laid the sure foundation for the Sinaitic legislation" (p. 110).

That seventh day which was singled out for Israel by the miracle of the manna in the Wilderness of Sin, and which was so kept before them for forty years, *that* was the identical seventh day which the word "formed in air by the power of the Eternal himself" declared to be the Sabbath of the Lord. And *that* was the very seventh day which that same word declared was the one on which God rested from creation, the day which he, at creation, blessed and sanctified. That was the only weekly Sabbath that was ever known to Moses or to Israel; and with its institution Moses had nothing whatever to do, either subtly or otherwise. And when Mr. Elliott brings in Christ as, "more subtly than Moses, yet as *really* . . . instituting a new Sabbath," it is simply saying, as a matter of fact, that Christ really instituted no new Sabbath at all. And that is the truth.

"That which he has asserted he had the power to do, we have the right to assume he has done," says Mr. Elliott. Is, then, the authority of the "Christian Sabbath" to rest upon assumption? Is the first day of the week to be brought in by an inference? The day that has received "the highest and strongest sanction possible even to Deity;" the day which has been specified in the word "formed in air by the power of the Eternal himself;" the day that was pointed out by weekly miracles for forty continuous years,—that is to be supplanted by one that is brought in merely upon the assumption that what the Lord has asserted that he had the power to do, he has done! But any such assumption is wholly illegitimate. And we shall prove by Mr. Elliott's own words that this, his assumption, is simply willful.

Christ said, "The Son of man is Lord even of the Sabbath day." Now in that declaration there is just as much of an assertion of his power to entirely set aside the Sabbath, as there is of his power to change it. Therefore, upon Mr. Elliott's proposition, there is just as much "right to assume" that Christ abolished the Sabbath, as there is to assume that he changed it. Mr. Elliott says: "As Lord of the Sabbath, he *doubtless had the power* to set it entirely aside." Therefore, if his assertion of his power to do a thing gives right to the assumption that he has done it, why is it not right to assume that he has set it entirely aside? But no; Mr. Elliott will not at all allow that. But in the very next sentence he says: "He had the right to change its day;" and, "That which he has asserted he had the power to do, we have the right to assume he has done," therefore the inference is that whatever change has come over it, was "by his authority and in fulfillment of his purpose."

We repeat, and this Mr. Elliott's argument allows, that in Christ's quoted words there is just as much assertion of the power to set the Sabbath "entirely aside," or do with it any imaginable thing, as there is to "change its day;" and Mr. Elliott's argument is just as sound a basis for the assumption that the Sabbath has been abolished, or that any other wild scheme has been accomplished with it, as it is for his assumption that it has been changed. And when Mr. Elliott lays down this proposition, which equally allows any assumption that the imagination might frame, it depends simply upon the wishes of the individual as to what shall be assumed, and therefore the assumption is wholly willful. Christ has asserted his power to call from their graves, all the dead; by Mr. Elliott's proposition we have the right to assume that he has done it. Christ has asserted his power to destroy death; under this novel proposition we have the right to assume that he has done it. Everybody knows, however, that such assumptions would be absolutely false; but they would be no more so than is Mr. Elliott's assumption that Christ changed the Sabbath. Mr. Elliott's proposition is simply absurd. The fact is that we have no right to assume anything in the premises.

Christ said: "When ye shall have done all those things which are commanded you, say, We are unprofitable servants; we have done that which was our duty to do." Luke 17:10. No man can do more than his duty. But when we have done all that is commanded, we have but done our duty. Therefore nothing can be duty that is not commanded. No man ever yet cited a commandment of God for keeping the first day of the week; there is no such commandment. Therefore until a commandment of God can be produced which enjoins the observance of the first day of the week, there can be no duty in that direction, Mr. Elliott's five-hundred-dollar-prize assumptions to the contrary, notwithstanding.

CHAPTER V.

"APOSTOLIC TESTIMONY."

In following the author of "The Abiding Sabbath" through the different principal headings under which his argument is framed, and his logic displayed, next after the "Testimony of Christ" we come to his so-called "Apostolic Testimony." Before we record his first definite proposition under this head, we wish to repeat one sentence from his exposition of the "Testimony of Christ:"—

"As Lord of the Sabbath, he doubtless had the power to set it entirely aside—a power which certainly he has *nowhere exercised, either by himself or through his apostles.*"—*P. 168.*

Here is the definite, positive statement that Christ has certainly nowhere exercised the power to set the Sabbath aside, either by himself or through his apostles. Now please read the following:—

"The Jewish Sabbath is definitely abolished by apostolic authority."—*P. 175.*

True, in this latter statement, he prefixes to the Sabbath the epithet "Jewish;" but on page 190 he defines the "Jewish" Sabbath to be the "seventh day." And as the Lord from Heaven said, "The seventh day is the Sabbath of the Lord thy God;" as that is the day upon which the Lord rested, which he blessed and which he sanctified; as from the creation of the world that was the only day that had ever been known as the Sabbath; and as that day is the only day that was ever recognized as the Sabbath, by either Christ or his apostles, his insertion of the epithet "Jewish" does not in the least relieve his latter statement from being a direct contradiction of the former. Therefore, as Christ nowhere set the Sabbath aside, "either by himself or through his apostles," and as the only weekly Sabbath of which either himself or his apostles knew anything "was definitely abolished by apostolic authority," it follows inevitably, by his own words, that if the apostles did abolish it, it was *without the authority of Christ.* But no, no; he will not allow that for an instant. Well, how does he avoid the conclusion? Oh, that is easy enough; he simply contradicts again both himself and the conclusion, thus:—

"It is demonstrated that the Sabbath of the law was abolished by apostolic authority, *in accordance with the developed teachings of Jesus Christ.*"—*P. 186.*

We beg our readers not to think that we draw out these sentences for the purpose of *making* contradictions, nor to think we are trying to make the matter worse than it really is. The contradictions are all there; we simply take them as we find them. And really we should not know how to go about it to make the thing worse than it is, nor as bad even as it is. We could wish indeed, that it were not so: but in such a cause it cannot be otherwise; and we want the people to see exactly how the Sunday institution is made to stand by an argument that ought to be the most conclusive, seeing it was considered worthy of a five-hundred-dollar prize.

We proceed. In proof of his word that the "Jewish" Sabbath is definitely abolished by apostolic authority, he says:—

"No wonder that the apostles could so little tolerate the proposed continuance of the bondage from which Christ had set them free. Gal. 5:1. Had he not taken away 'the handwriting of ordinances' against them, and 'nailed it to his cross?'"—*P. 176.*

But of all things the Sabbath is one that can by no possibility be classed with the ordinances that were *against* us. Christ said, "The Sabbath was made *for* man." The proof is absolute therefore that the Sabbath was no part of those ordinances which Paul says were "taken away;" for those that were taken away were such as were *against* us (Col. 2:14); unless, indeed, by Mr. Elliott's costly reasoning it could be made to appear that the same thing can be *for* us and *against* us at the same time. But, allowing all the wondrous efficacy of this high-priced logic, we doubt its power to the performance of this feat. Yet on the strength of the above statement he makes the following assertion:—

"With the ceremonial system vanished the Jewish Sabbath."—*P. 177.*

It would be an easy task indeed to disprove this, on

our own part; but he does it himself so effectually that we need merely to copy his words. Of the law given at Sinai, he says:—

"Of the law thus impressively given, the fourth commandment forms a part. Amid the same cloud of glory, the same thunders and lightnings, uttered by the same dread voice of the Infinite One, and graven by his finger, came forth these words as well: 'Remember the Sabbath day to keep it holy.' *It is impossible, in view of these facts, to class the Sabbath with the ceremonial institutions* of Israel. By the sacred seal of the divine lip and finger, it has been raised *far above those perishing rites."—P. 118.*

That is a fact. It *is* impossible, even by prefixing to it the epithet "Jewish," to class the Sabbath with the ceremonial institutions of Israel. For amid the same cloud of glory, the same thunderings and lightnings, the same dread voice of the Infinite One, who said, "Remember the Sabbath day to keep it holy," said also, "The *seventh day* is the Sabbath"—not of the Jews, but—"of *the Lord* thy God." It is indeed raised far above the perishing rites and ordinances that were against us. Therefore, although the ceremonial system vanished, the Sabbath remains; for it is no part of the ceremonial, but is an essential part of the moral system.

But Mr. Elliott is not done yet. He continues:—

"Such is the relation of apostolic teaching to the Jewish Sabbath. The yoke of the fathers with its crushing weight of sacerdotal requirements, was cast off. The galling fetters of tradition were broken, and forever was the infant church delivered from 'statutes that were not good, and judgments whereby they should not live.' Eze. 20:25."—*P. 180.*

Over against that please read this concerning the Sabbath of the fourth commandment:—

"It belongs to that moral law which Paul calls 'holy, and just, and good' (Rom. 7:12), and *not* that ritual law of which Peter declares, 'neither our fathers nor we were able to bear' it. Acts 15:10."—*Pp. 118, 119.*

So, then, the "yoke" which was "cast off" had nothing to do with the Sabbath; and the "statutes that were not good," etc., from which the infant church was delivered, were not at all those of which the Sabbath is a part, for they are "holy, and just, and good." And more, we should like to know upon what principle it is that the author of "The Abiding Sabbath" applies the phrase, "the galling fetters of tradition," to an institution given by the direct word of God, with a voice that shook the earth, and whose obligation was graven upon the tables of stone by the divine finger? For by the term "Jewish" Sabbath he invariably means the seventh day, and that is the very day named by the voice of God. But lo, this is to be pushed aside as "the galling fetters of tradition;" and in its place is to be put a day—Sunday—to which in all the word of God there is no shadow of sacredness attached; a day which rests for its authority solely upon, "we have the right to assume," "the right to infer," "doubtless," "probably," "in all likelihood," and "a religious *consensus* of the Christian church" (p. 203); and in all this we are to suppose there is nothing traditional!

Again we read:—

"It has already been shown that the Sabbath is a part of the moral law; it has the mark of universality as co-existent with man; it embodies a spiritual significance; it has a reasonable basis in the physical, mental and moral needs of man; it was incorporated in the decalogue, the outline of moral law given to Israel; it was enforced by such threatened penalties for violation and promised blessings for observance as *could not have been attached to a merely ceremonial ordinance;* and Jesus confirmed these historical and rational proofs by his own example and teachings."—*P. 183.*

That is the truth, and it is well stated. But now see what an extraordinary conclusion he draws from it:—

"Being, therefore, a part of the moral law, it is established as an apostolic institution by every word and phrase in which the apostles assert that law to be still binding on men."—*P. 184.*

"Being, therefore, a part of the moral law, it is established as an *apostolic* institution"!! Is, then, the moral law an apostolic institution? Does the moral law find its origin in the apostles? Do the precepts of the moral law find their spring in the will, and derive their authority from the actions, of the apostles? We confess it impossible for us to find language that would fittingly characterize such a preposterous proposition. It is astonishing how any man who is capable of forming the least conception of moral law, could set it forth as sober argument. Nor are we allowed to entertain the charitable view that perhaps it was done ignorantly; for Mr. Elliott himself has given us a perfect exposition of the ground of existence of moral law, not only of moral law in the abstract, but also of the Sabbath as being itself a moral institution. He says:—

"Suppose the question to be asked, How can we know that any precept is moral in its meaning and authority, and not simply a positive and arbitrary command? What better answer could be given to this inquiry than to say that *a moral precept must have the ground of its existence in the nature of God?* Our highest conception of the moral law is to regard it as *the transcript of his nature.* . . . All must agree that no more perfect vindication of the moral character of a law can be given than to show that it is a rule of the divine conduct; that it has been imposed upon his own activity by that infinite Will which is the supreme authority both in the physical and moral government of the universe. That law to which the Creator submits his own being must be of absolute binding force upon every creature made in his image. *Such is the law of the Sabbath.* 'God rested the seventh day,' and by so doing has given to the law of the Sabbath the highest and strongest sanction possible even to Deity."—*Pp. 23, 24.*

Such, in truth, is the origin and ground of authority of all moral obligation; such is the origin and ground of authority of the moral obligation of the seventh day. The seventh day is the only day that has, or ever has had, any such sanctions; therefore the seventh day is the only day that has, or that can have under the existing order of things, any claim whatever to the moral consideration of mankind. And the above statement of the ground of moral obligation effectually shows the utter absurdity of the idea that the Sabbath, "being a part of the moral law, is established as an *apostolic institution*." How could he possibly think himself called upon to make such a statement anyhow? Why, just thus: He has set out to have the first day of the week the Sabbath; he knows that it cannot be made to appear with any shadow of authority before the days of the apostles; he knows that even though it be made to originate with them, it can have no authority outside of the church unless it be moral; therefore, in contradiction of his own proofs, and in defiance of every principle of the basis of moral obligation, he is compelled to make the apostles the source of moral obligation. But he might better have spared himself the pains; for the idea is repugnant to the very consciousness of every man who will pause to think at all upon the subject. The apostles were the subjects, not the authors, of moral obligation.

Notice again that the statement which we are here discussing is the conclusion which he has drawn from a series of things which he says had "already been shown;" and we must give him the credit, which is very seldom his due, that from his main premises his conclusion is logical. The proposition under which he draws his conclusion is that, "The apostles, by confirming the moral law, have enforced the obligation of the Sabbath." Under this, his principal term is:—

"The apostles of Jesus Christ, as he had done in the sermon on the mount, re-enacted for the church the whole decalogue in its universal meanings."—*Pp. 181, 182.*

To enact, is "to decree; to establish by legal and authoritative acts; to make into a law."—*Webster.*

To re-enact, therefore, is to re-decree, to re-establish by legal and authoritative acts, to make again into a law. Now, if after the enactment by God and the re-enactment by Christ, the decalogue still needed to be confirmed by the apostles, and still needed legislative acts of the apostles to establish it legally and authoritatively as a moral standard, then we submit that Mr. Elliott's conclusion that the Sabbath, "being a part of the moral law, is established as an apostolic institution," is strictly logical. But we sincerely question the wisdom as well as the justice of paying five-hundred-dollar prizes for a style of reasoning which can be logical only in the reversal of every principle of the philosophy of moral obligation.

It most excellently serves his purpose though. His grand argument from "apostolic testimony" he closes thus:—

"As certainly as historical proof can be adduced for any fact, so certainly is it demonstrated that the Sabbath of the law was abolished by apostolic authority, in accordance with the developed teachings of Jesus Christ. But although the Sabbath of the law ceased, the law of the Sabbath is abiding."—*Pp. 185, 186.*

If, then, the Sabbath of the law be abolished while the **law of the Sabbath** remains, it must follow that the law of the Sabbath remains with no Sabbath. Oh, no, not at all. This is the emergency which he has all the while been laboring to create, and of course he meets it promptly. He continues thus :—

"And *it is in the highest degree probable* that the Lord's day which embodied its spirit was instituted by the immediate authority of the apostles, and therefore by the supreme authority of their Master, Jesus Christ."—*P. 186.*

And so the grand feat of getting Sunday into the fourth commandment is accomplished at last; and "it is in the highest degree probable" that the reader sees just how it is done. But there is yet one more thing to be done that the work may be complete in every part; that is, to transfer to the first day the Sabbath associations with which God has surrounded the seventh day. And we beg that Mr. Elliott be allowed to tell how that is done, because it rounds out his work in such symmetrical proportions. He says :—

"It is easy to comprehend how the Jewish Sabbath must almost at once have lost its hold on the affections of the disciples. . . . In the most powerful manner possible, those feelings of festal gladness and holy joy inseparable from the true idea of the Sabbath, were forever disconnected from the seventh day. . . . And *by the most natural revulsion of feeling, all* that was lost from the seventh day *was transferred* to the first day of the week."—*P. 188.*

There, the work is done; the climax is reached; the

"Hill Difficulty" is passed; and the first day of the week has become the "abiding Sabbath." It rests for its *authority* upon an, "it is in the highest degree probable;" and for its *sacredness*, upon "the most natural revulsion of feeling." But against all his probabilities of however high degree, and against all his revulsions of feeling however natural, we set the plain word of God "which liveth and *abideth* forever:" "The seventh day is the Sabbath of the Lord thy God; in it thou shalt not do any work."

CHAPTER VI.
"ORIGIN OF THE LORD'S DAY."

AFTER leading us through one hundred and eighty-six pages of fact and fiction, of truth and error, of contradiction and re-contradiction of Scripture, reason, and himself, the author of "The Abiding Sabbath" has arrived at the all-important conclusion that "it is in the *highest degree probable* that the Lord's day [Sunday] was instituted by the immediate authority of the apostles;" and that " by the most natural revulsion of feeling all that was lost from the seventh day was transferred to the first day of the week." And so after all this he comes to the discussion of the "origin of the Lord's day." Speaking of the resurrection of Christ, thus he proceeds:—

" The idea of completion, symbolized by the number seven and embodied in the Sabbath as the memorial of a finished creation, is transferred [by a " natural revulsion of feeling," we suppose, of course] to the Lord's day, the monument of a finished redemption."—*P. 189.*

If redemption had been finished when the Saviour arose from the dead, or were it even yet finished, we should question the right of Mr. Elliott, or any other man, to erect in memory of it a monument whose only foundation is a high degree of probability, and whose only rites of dedication are performed by a "natural revulsion of feeling." How much more may we question this right, when redemption, so far from being finished at the resurrection of Christ, will not be finished till the end of the world. The disciples asked the Saviour what should be the sign of his coming and of the end of the world, and he answered, "There shall be *signs* in the sun, and in the moon, and in the stars; and upon the earth distress of nations, with perplexity; the sea and the waves roaring; men's hearts failing them for fear, and for looking after those things which are coming on the earth; for the powers of heaven shall be shaken. And then shall they see the Son of man coming in a cloud with power and great glory. And when these things *begin* to come to pass, *then look up*, and lift up your heads; *for your redemption draweth nigh.*" Luke 21: 25–28. These things did not "begin to come to pass," till 1780 A. D.; for then it was that the sun was turned to darkness and the moon also. Therefore it is plain from these words of Christ, that instead of redemption being completed at the resurrection of Christ, it was not even "nigh" for 1749 years after that event.

This is confirmed by Paul. He says: "Ourselves also, which have the first-fruits of the Spirit, even we ourselves groan within ourselves, waiting for the adoption, to wit, the redemption of our body." Rom. 8:23. Our bodies will be redeemed at the resurrection of the dead: "I will ransom them from the power of the grave; I will redeem them from death" (Hos. 13:14); and the resurrection of the dead is accomplished at the second coming of the Lord. "For the Lord himself shall descend from Heaven with a shout, with the voice of the archangel, and with the trump of God; and the *dead in Christ shall rise* first; then *we which are alive* and remain *shall be caught up together with them* in the clouds to meet the Lord in the air; and so shall we ever be with the Lord." 1 Thess. 4:16, 17. Therefore Paul, in telling of our redemption, places its accomplishment exactly where Christ places it, that is, at the second coming of the Lord, and *not* at his resurrection.

Again Paul writes: "In whom [in Christ] ye also trusted, after that ye heard the word of truth, the gospel of your salvation; in whom also, after that ye believed, ye were sealed with that Holy Spirit of promise, which is the earnest of our inheritance until the redemption of the purchased possession." Eph. 1:13, 14. "That Holy Spirit of promise" was not given until the day of Pentecost, forty-nine days *after* the resurrection of Christ; and this, says Paul, is the earnest of our inheritance *until* (not because of) the *redemption* of the purchased possession. By this Holy Spirit, says Paul, "ye are sealed *unto* the day of redemption." Eph. 4:30. Now as the Holy Spirit was given to be with those who trust in Christ "*until* the redemption," and as that Spirit was not so given till forty-nine days *after* the resurrection of Christ, this is proof most positive that the day of the resurrection of Christ could not possibly be made "the monument of a finished redemption." And when Mr. Elliott, or anybody else, whether individually or by " a general *consensus* of the Christian church," sets up the first day of the week as a monument of a finished redemption, it simply perverts the Scripture doctrine of redemption, and puts darkness for light, and error for truth.

Again he says of the first day of the week:—

"*It is the abiding Sabbath.* It was on the first day of the week that the Saviour rose. It is remarkable that this phrase, 'first day of the week,' marks the only case in which any day of the week is distinguished from the rest in Scripture by its number, excepting the seventh day, or Jewish Sabbath. Eight times the term is used in the New Testament, five of the instances occurring in connection with the account of the Lord's resurrection. Other days have no distinctive title, save only the sixth day, which is the 'Sabbath eve,' or 'day of preparation.' The first day is therefore placed in such significant relation with the seventh day as to impress upon it a meaning which cannot be disregarded."—*Pp. 189, 190.*

If the mention of the first day of the week *eight* times in the New Testament marks it so distinctively and impresses upon it so strong a meaning as Mr. Elliott imagines, how is it that the mention of the Sabbath *fifty-nine* times in the New Testament (with sole reference to the seventh day) can impress upon it no meaning whatever? It would seem that if the mention of a day would give any distinction at all to it, the day that is mentioned most would properly be entitled to the most distinction. But behold, here it is just the reverse; the day that is mentioned eight times is entitled to the distinction, while a day that is mentioned *more than seven times as often* is entitled to no distinction whatever!

He remarks the "significant relations" in which the first day of the week is placed with the seventh, but in not one instance does he notice these relations. We shall do it for him; for there is a relation there which is very "significant" indeed, in view of his theory that the first day of the week is "the abiding Sabbath."

The first mention of the first day of the week in the New Testament is in Matt. 28 : 1 : "In the end of the Sabbath, as it began to dawn toward the first day of week, came Mary Magdalene and the other Mary to see the sepulcher." There *is* a "significant" relation between the Sabbath—the seventh day—and the first day of the week; and that which is signified by it is that the Sabbath is ended before the first day of the week begins.

The next mention is in Mark 16 : 1, 2 : "And when the Sabbath was past, Mary Magdalene, and Mary the mother of James, and Salome, had bought sweet spices, that they might come and anoint him. And very early in the morning, the first day of the week, they came unto the sepulcher at the rising of the sun." Here also is a very significant relation between the Sabbath and the first day of the week; and the significance of it is that the Sabbath is *past* before the first day of the week comes. Notice, too, that these women came to the sepulcher *very early* in the morning the first day of the week; yet as early as it was, "*the Sabbath was past.*" And the significance of that is, that Mr. Elliott, or anyone else, may arise *very early in the morning* the first day of the week, just as early as he pleases in fact, but he will be too late for the Sabbath—he will find that the Sabbath is past; it will not "abide" on the first day of the week.

The third mention is Luke 23:54–56; 24:1: "And that day [the day of crucifixion] was the preparation, and the Sabbath drew on. And the women also, which came with him from Galilee, followed after, and beheld the sepulcher, and how his body was laid. And they returned, and prepared spices and ointments; and rested the Sabbath day according to the commandment. Now upon the first day of the week, very early in the morning, they came unto the sepulcher, bringing the spices which they had prepared, and certain others with them." In this passage, the "relations" between the Sabbath and the first day of the week are doubly significant. For here it is not only shown that the Sabbath is past before the first day of the week comes; it is not only shown that although people may arise very early in the morning the first day of the week, they will be too late for the Sabbath; but it is stated explicitly that the Sabbath that was past was "the Sabbath day *according to the commandment.*" Therefore it is by these texts proved as absolutely as the word of God can prove anything, that Sunday, the first day of the week, the so-called Lord's day, is *not* the Sabbath according to the commandment of God; and that when people rest on Sunday, the first day of the week, they do *not* rest "according to the commandment." It is likewise proved that the Sabbath according to the commandment is—not a seventh part of time, nor simply one day in seven, but—the definite seventh day of the week, the day *before* the one on which Christ rose from the dead.

We repeat: the relations in which are placed the seventh day and the first, in the Scripture, are indeed most "significant,"—so significant that it is utterly impossible to honestly or truthfully pass off the first day of the week as the Sabbath; and that it proves positively that the day before that upon which Christ arose from the dead, the day before the first day of the week, is the Sabbath according to the commandment of God; and that therefore the seventh day, and *not* the first, is "the abiding Sabbath."

But our author continues:—

"After the several appearances of the Saviour on the day of his resurrection, there is no recorded appearance until a week later, when the first day is again honored by the Master. John 20:26. The exact mention of the time, which is not usual even with John's exactness, very evidently implies that there was already attached a special significance to the 'first day of the week' at the time when this gospel was written."—*P. 190.*

From Mr. Elliott's assertion of "the *exact* mention

of the time, which is not usual even with John's exactness," it would naturally be supposed that John 20:26 makes exact mention of the first day of the week; we might expect to open the book and read there some such word as, "the next first day of the week," etc. Now let us read the passage referred to, and see how much exactness of expression there is about the first day of the week. The record says: "And after eight days again his disciples were within, and Thomas with them; then came Jesus, the doors being shut, and stood in the midst, and said, Peace be unto you." John 20:26.

There is the "exact mention" which attaches significance to the first day of the week! That is, an expression in which the first day of the week is not mentioned; an expression, indeed, in which there is no exactness at all, but which is wholly indefinite. "*After* eight days" is exactly the phrase which John wrote. Will Mr. Elliott tell us exactly how long after? Granting that it was the very next day after eight days, then we would ask the author of the "Abiding Sabbath" if the first day of the week comes every *ninth* day? If this is to be considered an exact mention of time, unusual even with John's exactness, then we should like to see a form of words which Mr. Elliott would consider *inexact*.

Perhaps some one may ask what day *we* think it was. We make no pretensions to wisdom above that which is written. And as the word of God says it was "*after* eight days," without telling us anything about how long after, we know nothing more definitely about what day it was than what the word tells us, that it was "after eight days." We know of a similar expression in Matt. 17:1: "And *after six days* Jesus taketh Peter, James, and John his brother, and bringeth them up into an high mountain apart;" and we know that Luke's record of the same scene says: "And it came to pass *about an eight days* after these sayings, he took Peter, and John, and James, and went up into a mountain to pray." Luke 9:28. Therefore we know that Inspiration shows that "after six days" is "about eight days," and by the same rule "after eight days" is about ten days. But even then it is as indefinite as it was before, and Inspiration alone knows what day it was.

But, though we know nothing at all about what day it was, we do know what day it was *not*. We know that the meeting previous to the one under consideration was on the first day of the week, John 20:19. We know that the next first day of the week would come exactly a week from that time. We know that a week consists of exactly seven days. And as the word of God says plainly that this meeting was "after *eight* days," we therefore know by the word of God that this meeting was *not* on the next first day of the week.

What saith the Scripture about the first day of the week? And what was the purpose of the Saviour's repeated appearances on the day of his resurrection? Let us see.

1. "In the end of the Sabbath, as it began to dawn toward the first day of the week, came Mary Magdalene and the other Mary to see the sepulcher." Matt. 28:1. Here all that is said is, that two women went to the sepulcher on the first day of the week. Well, what reason for keeping the first day of the week lies in that fact? None whatever.

2. "And when the Sabbath was past, Mary Magdalene, and Mary the mother of James, and Salome, had bought sweet spices, that they might come and anoint him. And very early in the morning, the first day of the week, they came unto the sepulcher at the rising of the sun." Mark 16:1, 2. Can anybody tell what there is about this text that shows that the first day of the week is the Sabbath? How can the first day of the week be the Sabbath, and yet the Sabbath be past before the first day of the week begins?

3. "Now upon the first day of the week, very early in the morning, they [the women who came from Galilee] came unto the sepulcher, bringing the spices which they had prepared, and certain others with them." Luke 24:1

4 "The first day of the week cometh Mary Magdalene early, when it was yet dark, unto the sepulcher and seeth the stone taken away from the sepulcher." John 20:1.

Notice that these four statements—one by each of the Gospel writers—are not four records of four distinct things, but four distinct records of *the same* thing, and the same time, even the same hour. Each one tells what occurred in the morning of a certain first day of the week, and the only fact stated in all four of the records, about the first day of the week, is that certain women came to the sepulcher very early in the morning. Then what is there in all this upon which to base any reason for keeping the first day of the week? Nothing.

In the Gospels there is mention made of the first day of the week only twice more. These are in Mark and John. And the record in John and the close of the record in Mark speak of the same time precisely, only it is in the evening, whereas, the other was in the morning of that same first day of the week.

5. Here is Mark's record: "Now when Jesus was risen early the first day of the week he appeared first to Mary Magdalene, out of whom he had cast seven devils. And she went and told them that had been with him, as they mourned and wept. And they, when they had heard that he was alive, and had been seen of her, believed not. After that he appeared in another form unto two of them [Luke 24:13-48], as they walked, and went into the country. And they went and told it unto the residue; neither believed they them. Afterward he appeared unto the eleven as they sat at meat, and upbraided them with their unbelief and hardness of heart, because they believed not them which had seen him after he was risen." Mark 16:9-14.

6. Of this same time John says: "Then the same day at evening, being the first day of the week, when

the doors were shut where the disciples were assembled for fear of the Jews, came Jesus and stood in the midst, and saith unto them, Peace be unto you. And when he had so said, he showed unto them his hands and his side. Then were the disciples glad, when they saw the Lord." John 20 : 19, 20.

Here, then, are all the instances in which the term "first day of the week" is used in the Gospels, and the manifest story is simply this: When the Sabbath was past, the women came to the sepulcher very early in the morning on the first day of the week, and found the stone rolled away from the sepulcher, and Jesus risen. Then Jesus appeared to Mary Magdalene, and she went and told the disciples that *Jesus was risen* and they "believed not." Then Jesus appeared to two of the disciples themselves as they went into the country, and they went and told it to the others, who yet believed not. Then Jesus appeared to all the company together and upbraided them with their unbelief and hardness of heart because they had not believed them which had seen him after he was risen, then showed them his hands, and his feet, and his side, and said: "Behold my hands and my feet, that it is I myself; handle me, and see. . . . Have ye here any meat? And they gave him a piece of a broiled fish, and of an honeycomb. And he took it, and did eat before them." Luke 24 : 39–43.

Now take this whole narrative from beginning to end and where is there a word in it that conveys any idea that anybody ever kept the first day of the week, or that it ever should be kept as the Sabbath or for any other sacred or religious purpose whatever? Just nowhere at all. The Scriptures throughout show that the purpose of the repeated appearances of Jesus was not to institute a new Sabbath, for there is not one word said about it, *but to convince his disciples that he really was risen, and was alive again, that they might be witnesses to the fact.* The words above quoted show this, but Thomas was not there with the others, and he still did not believe, and so at another time, "after eight days," Thomas was with them, and Jesus came again for the express purpose of convincing him, for he simply said to the company, "Peace be unto you," and then spoke directly to Thomas, saying: "Reach hither thy finger, and behold my hands; and reach hither thy hand, and thrust it into my side; and be not faithless, but believing." John 20 : 24–27.

This is made positive by the words of Peter: "Him God raised up the third day, and *showed him openly; not to all the people, but unto witnesses chosen before of God, even to us, who did eat and drink with him after he rose from the dead.*" Acts 10 : 40, 41. "This Jesus hath God raised up, *whereof we all are witnesses.*" Acts 2 : 32. And that evening of the day of his resurrection, when he said to the eleven to handle him and see that it was he, and when he ate the piece of broiled fish and of a honeycomb, he said to them, "Thus it is written, and thus it behooved Christ to suffer, and *to rise from the dead* the third day; . . . and *ye are witnesses* of these things." Luke 24 : 46–48.

Once more, Peter said, Ye "killed the Prince of life, whom *God hath raised from the dead;* whereof *we are witnesses.*" Acts 3:15.

They were witnesses that Christ was risen from the dead because a living Saviour, and faith in a living Saviour, alone could be preached. How did they become such witnesses? Christ showed himself to them, and "did eat and drink with them after he rose from the dead." Then what was the purpose of his appearances on this first day of the week mentioned in the four Gospels, and his appearance to Thomas afterward? To give them "*infallible proofs*" that he was "alive after his passion." Acts 1:3. Then where does the first-day-of-the-week Sabbath come in? Nowhere. In these texts, in the four Gospels, which speak of the first day of the week, where is there conveyed any idea that that day shall be kept as the Sabbath? Nowhere.

Then says Mr. Elliott:—

"These repeated appearances of Jesus upon the first day *doubtless* furnished the first suggestion of the practice which very quickly sprang up in the church of employing that day for religious assembly and worship. . . . This impression *must have been* strongly intensified by the miraculous occurrences of Pentecost, *if* that festival fell, as we think *probable*, on the first day of the week—a view maintained by the early tradition of the church and by many eminent scholars." —*Pp. 190, 191.*

Yes, "doubtless" it "must have been," "if" it was as he thinks "probable." But against the "early tradition of the church," and the "many eminent scholars," we will place just as many and as eminent scholars, and the word of God. It is true that the day of the week on which that Pentecost came is not of the least importance in itself either for or against any sacredness that was put upon it by that occurrence. It is "the day of Pentecost" that is named by the word of God. It was the feast of Pentecost with its types, that was to meet the grand object—the reality—to which its services had ever pointed. And everybody knows that the Pentecost came on each day of the week in succession as the years passed by; the same as does Christmas, or the Fourth of July, or any other yearly celebration. Therefore whatever were its occurrences, they could have no purpose in giving to the day of the week on which it fell any particular significance.

Yet though this be true, there is so much made of it by those who will have the first day of the week to be the Sabbath, by claiming always that Pentecost was on the first day of the week, that we feel disposed to refer to the Scriptures, which show that this claim is not founded on fact.

The word Pentecost signifies "*the fiftieth day,*" and was always counted, beginning with the sixteenth day of the first month. It is also called "the feast of weeks," because it was seven complete weeks from the day of the offering of the first-fruits, which was the second day of the feast of unleavened bread, the sixteenth day of the first month. On the fourteenth day of the first month, all leaven was to be put away from all the houses.

They were to kill the passover lamb in the evening of the fourteenth, and with it, at the beginning of the fifteenth day of the month, they were to begin to eat the unleavened bread, and the feast of unleavened bread was to continue until the twenty-second day of the month. The first day of the feast, that is, the fifteenth of the month, was to be a sabbath, no servile work was to be done in that day. Ex. 12: 6-8, 15-19: Lev. 23: 5-7. Because of the putting away of the leaven on the fourteenth day, and the beginning to eat the unleavened bread on the evening of that day, it is sometimes referred to as the first day of unleavened bread; but the fifteenth day was really the first, and was the one on which no servile work was to be done.

On "the *morrow*" *after* this fifteenth day of the month—this sabbath—the wave-sheaf of the first-fruits was to be offered before the Lord, and with that day—the sixteenth day of the month—they were to begin to count fifty days, and when they reached the fiftieth day that was *Pentecost*. Lev. 23: 10, 11, 15, 16; Deut. 16: 8, 9. Now if we can learn on what day of the week the passover fell at the time of the crucifixion, we can tell on what day of the week the Pentecost came that year. We know that the Saviour was crucified "the day before the Sabbath." Mark 15.42. We know that the Sabbath was "the Sabbath day according to the commandment" (Luke 23: 54-56), and *that* was the seventh day—Saturday—and therefore "the day before," was the sixth day—Friday. It is plain, then, that Jesus was crucified on

Friday; this in itself, requires no proof, but it is important to distinctly mention it here, because the day before he was crucified, "the disciples came to Jesus, saying unto him, Where wilt thou that we *prepare for thee to eat the passover?* And he said, Go into the city to such a man, and say unto him, The Master saith, My time is at hand; I will keep the passover at thy house with my disciples. And the disciples did as Jesus had appointed them; *and they made ready the passover.*" Matt. 26:17-19; Mark 14:12-16; Luke 22:7-15. And *that* was the evening of Thursday, the fourteenth day of the month; because "the fourteenth day of the month at even is the Lord's passover." Lev. 23:5; Ex. 12:6.

From that passover supper Jesus went direct to Gethsemane, whence he was taken by the mob which Judas had brought, and after his shameful treatment by the priests and Pharisees and soldiers, was crucified in the afternoon of the same day. That was *the fifteenth day of the month*, the first day of the feast of unleavened bread; and the morrow after that day was the *first* of the fifty days which reached to Pentecost. Therefore, as the day of the crucifixion was the first day of the feast of unleavened bread, and was Friday, the fifteenth day of the month; and as the next day, the sixteenth of the month, was the Sabbath according to the commandment, and was the *first* of the fifty days; anyone who will count the fifty days will find for himself that "the fiftieth day," Pentecost, fell that year on "the Sabbath day according to the commandment," and *that* is the seventh day.

So then the day which the advocates of Sunday sacredness claim has received such sacred sanctions by the occurrences of the day of Pentecost, was not the first day of the week at all; but it was the seventh day, the very day which they so unsparingly condemn. (See Geikie's "Life of Christ," Smith's "Dictionary of the Bible," and the opinions of such men as Neander, Olshausen, Dean Alford, Lightfoot, Jennings, Professor Hackett, Albert Barnes, etc.) Let us say again that we make no use of this fact in the way of claiming any sacredness for the seventh day because of it; that day, in the beginning, was given "the highest and strongest sanction possible even to Deity," and nothing was ever needed afterward to add to its sacredness. We simply state it as the truth according to the Scriptures; and being, as it is, the truth, it shows that the claims for Sunday sacredness based upon the occurrences of Pentecost are entirely unfounded.

CHAPTER VII.

"APOSTOLIC EXAMPLE," OR CHRIST'S EXAMPLE?
ACTS 20:7.

IN continuing his search for the origin of the first day of the week as the Lord's day, the author of "The Abiding Sabbath" comes to Acts 20:7. As this text mentions a meeting of disciples on the first day of the week, at which an apostle preached, it is really made the foundation upon which to lay the claim of the custom of the primitive church, and the example of the apostles in sanctioning the observance of Sunday as the Sabbath. But although there was a meeting held on the first day of the week, and although an apostle was at the meeting, as a matter of fact, there is in it neither custom nor example in favor of keeping Sunday as the Sabbath. Here is what Mr. Elliott makes of the passage:—

"The most distinct reference to the Christian use of the first day of the week is that found in Acts 20:7: 'And upon the first day of the week, when the disciples came together to break bread, Paul preached unto them.' . . . The language clearly implies that the apostle availed himself of the occasion brought about by the custom of assemblage on the first day of the week to preach to the people. . . . Here, then, is a plain record of the custom of assemblage on the first day of the week, less than thirty years after the resurrection. The language is just what would be used in such a case."—*Pp. 194, 195.*

It is hard to see how he can find "a plain record of the custom of assemblage on the first day of the week," when the record says nothing at all about any such custom. In all the narrative of which this verse forms a part there is no mention whatever of anything that was there done being done according to custom, nor to introduce what should become a custom, nor that it was to be an example to be followed by Christians throughout all coming time. So the fact is that Mr. Elliott's "plain record" of a custom lacks the essential thing which would show a custom.

Nor is his statement that "the language is just what would be used in such a case," any more in accordance with the fact; for when Luke, who wrote this record, had occasion to speak of that which was a custom he did so plainly. For example: "And he [Jesus] came to Nazareth, where he had been brought up; and, *as his custom was*, he went into the synagogue on the Sabbath day, and stood up for to read." Luke 4:16. Again: "And Paul, *as his manner* [custom] *was*, went in unto them, and three Sabbath days reasoned with them out of the Scriptures." Acts 17:2. In these two passages, the words, "as his custom was," and "as his manner was," as Luke wrote them, are identical—*Kata to eiōthos*—and in both instances mean precisely *as his custom* was; and *that* "language is just what" Inspiration *has* used in such cases as a plain record of a custom. Therefore we submit that the total absence of any such language from the passage under consideration, is valid argument that it is not a record of any such thing as the *custom* of the assemblage of Christians on the first day of the week.

If the record really said that it was then a custom to assemble on the first day of the week; if it said: Upon the first day of the week, when the disciples came together, *as their custom was,* as the same writer says that it was the custom of Christ and of Paul to go to the Sabbath assemblies; if it said: Upon the first day of the week Paul preached to the disciples *as his custom was;* then no man could deny that such was indeed the custom: but as in the word of God there is neither statement nor hint to that effect, no man can rightly affirm that such was a custom, without going beyond the word of God; and *that* is prohibited by the word itself—"Thou shalt not add thereto, nor diminish from it." Deut. 12:32. More than this, reading into that passage the "custom" of assemblage on the first day of the week, is not only to go beyond that which is written; it is to do violence to the very language in which it is written. The meaning of the word "custom" is, "A frequent repetition of the same act." A single act is not custom. An act repeated once or twice is not custom. The *frequent* repetition of an act, *that* is custom. Now as Acts 20:7 is the *only* case on record that a religious meeting was ever held, either by the disciples or the apostles, on the first day of the week, as there is no record of a *single* repetition of that act, much less of a "frequent repetition" of it, it follows inevitably that there is no shadow of justice nor of right in the claim that the custom of the apostles and of the primitive church sanctions the observance of that day as the day of rest and worship—the Sabbath. There was no such custom.

We have a few words more to say on this passage, and that we may discuss it with the best advantage to the reader we copy the whole connection:—

"And upon the first day of the week, when the disciples came together to break bread, Paul preached unto them, ready to depart on the morrow; and continued his speech until midnight. And there were many lights in the upper chamber, where they were gathered together. And there sat in a window a certain young man named Euytchus, being fallen into a deep sleep; and as Paul was long preaching, he sunk down with sleep, and fell down from the third loft, and was taken up dead. And Paul went down, and fell on him, and embracing him said, Trouble not yourselves; for his life is in him. When he therefore was come up again, and had broken bread, and eaten, and talked a long while, even till break of day, so he departed." Verses 7-11.

Upon the face of this whole narrative it is evident that this meeting was at night. Let us put together several of the statements: (1) "Upon the first day of the week when the disciples *came together* . . . there were *many lights* in the upper chamber, *where they were gathered together.*" (2) "Paul *preached* unto them . . . and continued his speech *until midnight.*" (3) At midnight Eutychus fell out of the window, and Paul went down and brought him up, and *then* he broke the bread and ate, therefore we may read, "The disciples came together to break bread," and *after midnight* the bread was broken. (4) *After that* Paul "talked a long while, even *till break of day*, so he departed." Therefore we may read, (5) Upon the first day of the week, the disciples came together, and there were many lights where they were gathered together. They came together to break bread, and after midnight the bread was broken. Paul preached unto them until midnight, and even till break of day. When the disciples came together, Paul was ready to depart on the morrow, and when he had talked a long while, even till break of day, so he departed. There can be no room for any reasonable doubt that the meeting referred to in Acts 20: 7 was wholly a night meeting, and not only that but that it was an *all*-night meeting.

This meeting being therefore in the night of the first day of the week, the question properly arises, According to the Bible, what part of the complete day does the night form? Is the night the first or the last part of the complete day? The Bible plainly shows that the night is the first part of the day. There was darkness on the earth before there was light. When God created the world, *darkness* was upon the face of the deep. Then "God said, Let there be light;

and there was light." Then "God called the light day, and the darkness he called night." As the darkness was called night, as the darkness was upon the earth before the light, and as it takes both the night and the day—the darkness and the light—to make the complete day, it follows that in the true count of days by the revolution of the earth, the night precedes the day. This is confirmed by the Scripture: "The evening [the darkness, the night] and the morning [the light, the day] were the first day."

This is the order which God established in the beginning of the world; it is the order that is laid down in the beginning of the book of God; and it is the order that is followed throughout the book of God. In Leviticus 23:27–32, giving directions about the day of atonement, God said that it should be "the tenth day of the seventh month," and that that was from the ninth day of the month at even; "from even unto even, shall ye celebrate your sabbath." Thus the tenth day of the month began in the evening of the ninth day of the month. And so according to Bible time every day begins in the evening, and evening is at the going down of the sun. Deut. 16:6. Therefore as the meeting mentioned in Acts 20:7–11 was in the night of the first day of the week, and as in the word and the order of God the night is the first part of the day, it follows that that meeting was on what is now called Saturday night. For if it had been on what is now called Sunday night it would have been on the second day of the week and not on the first. So Conybeare and Howson, in "Life and Epistles of Paul," say: "It was the evening which succeeded the Jewish Sabbath." And that is now called Saturday night.

This meeting, then, being on what is now called Saturday night, as Paul preached till midnight, and after the breaking of bread talked till break of day and departed, it follows that at break of day on the first day of the week, at break of day on Sunday, Paul started afoot from Troas to Assos, a distance of twenty miles, with the intention of going on board a ship at Assos and continuing his journey, which he did. For says the record: "We [Paul's companions in travel, Acts 20: 4] went before to ship, and sailed unto Assos, there intending to take in Paul; for so had he appointed, minding himself to go afoot. And when he met with us at Assos, we took him in, and came to Mitylene." Verses 13, 14. Paul not only walked from Troas to Assos on Sunday, but he *appointed* that his companions should sail to that place —about forty miles by water—and be there by the time he came so that he could go on without delay. And when he reached Assos he went at once aboard the ship and sailed away to Mitylene, which was nearly forty miles further. That is to say, on the first day of the week Paul walked twenty miles and then sailed nearly forty more, making nearly sixty miles that he traveled; and he *appointed* that his companions—Luke, Timothy, Tychicus, Trophimus, Gaius, Aristarchus, and Secundus—should sail forty miles and then take him aboard, and all sail nearly forty miles more, making nearly eighty miles travel for them, all on Sunday. And this is exactly how these Christians kept that first day of the week of which mention is made in Acts 20.

But nowadays men try to make it appear that it is an awful sin to travel on Sunday. Yes, some people now seem to think that if a ship should sail on Sunday, the sin would be so great that nothing but a perfect miracle of grace would keep it from sinking. Paul neither taught nor acted any such thing, for says the record: "We went before to ship, and sailed; . . . for *so had he appointed.*" Paul and his companions regarded Sunday in nowise different from the other common working days of the week. For, mark, the first day of the week they sailed from Troas to Mitylene, "the next day" they sailed from Mitylene to Chios, "the next day" from Chios to Samos and Trogyllium, and "the next day" to Miletus. Here are "the first day of the week," "the next day," "the next day," and "the next day," and Paul and his companions did the same things on one of these days that they did on another. They considered one of them no more sacred than another. They considered the first day of the week to be no more of a sabbath than the next day, or the next day, or the next day. True, Paul preached all night, before he started on the first day of the week; but on the fifth or sixth day of the week he preached also at Miletus, to the elders of the church of Ephesus.

Instead, therefore, of the Sunday deriving any sacredness from the word of God, or resting for its observance upon the authority of that word, or upon that which is just and right, or upon the example of the apostles, or the custom of the primitive church, it is contrary to all these. It is essentially an interloper, and rests for its so-called sacredness and for its authority upon nothing but "the commandments of men."

Of all the arguments that are made in support of the first day of the week as the Sabbath, or Lord's day, the one which above all is the most thoroughly sophistical and deceptive is this that proposes to rest its obligation upon "the example of the apostles," or of the "primitive Christians." We want to look into this thing a little and see what the claim is worth, upon its own merits. "The example of the apostles." What is it? If the phrase means anything at all, it means that the example of the apostles is the standard of human duty in moral things. But if that be so, their example must be the standard in every other duty as well as in the supposed duty of keeping the first day of the week. But nobody ever thinks of appealing to the example of the apostles in any question of morals, except in the (supposed moral) matter of the observance of the first day of the week as a sacred day. By this, therefore, even those who make the claim of apostolic example do, in effect, deny the very claim which they themselves set up.

Who ever thinks of resting upon the example of the apostles, the obligation to obey any one of the ten commandments? Take the first commandment, "Thou shalt have no other gods before me." Who ever thinks of appealing to the example of the apostles in impressing upon men the obligation to obey this? And what should be thought of a person anyhow who would do it? That commandment is the will of God, and the basis of its obligation is as much higher than the example of the apostles as Heaven is higher than earth, or as God is higher than man. And the obligation to obey that commandment rested just as strongly upon the apostles as it ever did, or as it ever will, upon anybody else.

It is so with every commandment of the decalogue, and with every form of duty under any one of the commandments. Who would think of impressing upon children the duty to honor their parents by citing them to the example of the apostles? The duty to honor parents possesses higher sanctions than the example of the apostles, even the sanctions of the will of God. And to inculcate upon the minds of children this duty, upon the basis of the example of the apostles, would only be to turn them away from God, and would destroy all the force of this duty upon the conscience. It is so in relation to every moral precept. The apostles were subjects and not masters of moral obligation. Moral duties spring from the will of God, and not from the example of men; and a knowledge of moral duties is derivable alone from the commands of God, and not from the actions of men; all of which goes to show that in point of morals there is no such thing as apostolic example. This is shown by other considerations as well. In fact every consideration only the more fully demonstrates it.

The law of God—the ten commandments—is the supreme standard of morals for the universe, and so expresses the whole duty of man. That law is perfect, and demands perfection in every subject of it. Therefore, whoever would be an example to men in the things pertaining to the law of God, that is, in any moral duty, must be perfect. Whoever would be an example to men in moral duties must not only *be* perfect, but he must have always been perfect. He must always have met to the full every requirement of the law of God. But this no *man* whom the world ever saw has done. "For all have sinned and come short of the glory of God." "They are all gone out of the way." The perfection of the law of God has never been met in any man whom the world ever saw. Therefore, no man whom the world ever saw can ever be an example to men in moral duties. Consequently there is not, and there never can be, any such thing as apostolic example in moral things. To many this may appear to be stating the case too strongly, because the apostles were inspired men. We abate not one jot from the divine inspiration of the apostles, nor from the respect justly due them as inspired men; but we say without the slightest hesitation that, although the apostles were indeed inspired, they are not examples to men in moral duties. Because, first, no degree of inspiration can ever put a man above the law of God; and because, secondly, although we know that the doctrine and the writings of the apostles are inspired, yet we know also that all their *actions were not* inspired. This we know because the inspired record tells us so. Here is the inspired record of one instance in point: "When Peter was come to Antioch, I withstood him to the face, *because he was to be blamed.* For before that certain came from James, he did eat with the Gentiles; but when they were come, he withdrew and separated himself, fearing them which were of the circumcision. And the other Jews dissembled likewise with him; insomuch that Barnabas also was carried away with their dissimulation. But when I saw that they *walked not uprightly* according to the truth of the gospel, I said unto Peter before them all," etc. Gal. 2:11–14.

Peter "was to be blamed." He "walked not uprightly according to the truth of the gospel." Then what kind of "apostolic example" was that to follow? and where were those led who followed it? They were being carried away with *dissimulation*— two-facedness, hypocrisy; they were being led away from "the truth of the gospel." But they could claim apostolic example for it, and that too with the very apostles—Peter and Barnabas—present, whom they might claim as their examples. But God did not leave them there; he rebuked their sin, and corrected their fault, and brought them back from their blameworthiness to uprightness once more according to the truth of the gospel. And in the record of it God has shown all men that there is no such thing as "apostolic example" for anybody to follow, but that the truth of the gospel and the word of God is that according to which all men must walk.

Another instance, and in this even Paul himself was involved: "Paul said unto Barnabas, Let us go again and visit our brethren in every city where we have preached the word of the Lord, and see how they do. And Barnabas determined to take with them John, whose surname was Mark. But Paul thought not good to take him with them, who departed from them from Pamphylia, and went not with them to the work. And the contention was so sharp between them, that they departed asunder one from the other." Acts 15 : 36-39.

"The *contention* was so *sharp* between them." Is that "apostolic example" which is to be followed by all men? Everybody will at once say, No. But why is it not? Because it is not right. But when we say that that is not right, in that very saying we at once declare that there is a standard by which the apostles themselves must be tried, and by which their example must be measured. And that is to acknowledge at once that there is no such thing as "apostolic example."

We do not cite these things to reproach the apostles, nor to charge them with not being Christians. They were men of like passions with all the rest of us; and were subject to failings as well as all the rest of us. They had weaknesses in themselves to strengthen by exercise in divine grace, and defects of moral character to overcome by the help of God. They had to fight the good fight of faith as well as all the rest of us. And they fought the good fight and became at last "more than conquerors through Him that hath loved" them as well as us, and hath washed us all "from our sins in his own blood." Far be it that we should cite these things to reproach the apostles; we simply bring forth the record which God has given of the apostles, to show to men that if they will be perfect they must have a higher aim than "the example of the apostles." By these things from the word of God we would show to men that, in working out the problem of human destiny under the perfect law of God, that problem must be worked by an example that never fails. We write these things not that we love the apostles less, but Christ more. And this is only what the apostles themselves have shown. Ask the apostles whether we shall follow them as examples. Peter, shall we follow your example? Answer: "Christ also suffered for us, leaving us *an example,* that *ye* should follow *his steps; who did no sin,* neither was guile found in his mouth." 1 Peter 2: 21, 22. Paul, shall we not follow your example? Answer: "Be ye followers of me, *even as I also am of Christ.*" 1 Cor. 11:1. John, "that disciple whom Jesus loved," shall we not follow your example? Shall we not walk in your ways? Answer: "He that saith he abideth in Him, ought himself also so to walk, even as He walked." 1 John 2:6. Wherefore, as the apostles themselves repudiate the claim of apostolic example, it follows that there is no such thing as "the example of the apostles."

Jesus Christ is the one only example for men to follow. To every man he commands absolutely, "Follow me." "Take *my* yoke upon you and *learn of me.*" "I am the door." "He that entereth not by the door into the sheepfold, but climbeth up some other way [by the "other way" of apostolic example, for instance], the same is a thief and a robber." "By *me* if any man enter in, he shall be saved." The Lord Jesus is the one only person whom this world ever saw who met perfectly every requirement of the perfect law of God. He was made flesh, and he, in the flesh, and form, and nature of man, stood in every place and met every temptation that any man can ever meet, and in every place and in everything he met all the demands of the perfect law of God. He did it from infancy to the prime of manhood, and never failed. "He was tempted in all points like as we are, yet without sin." Therefore, as he is the only person whom this world ever saw who ever met to the full all the perfect requirements of the law of God, it follows that he is the only person whom the world ever saw, or ever shall see, who can be an example for men, or whose example is worthy to be followed by men.

Therefore, when preachers and leaders of theological thought anywhere present before men any other example, even though it be the example of the apostles, and seek to induce men to follow any other example, even though it be proposed as apostolic example, such conduct is sin against God, and treason against our Lord Jesus Christ. And that there are men in this day, Protestants too, who are doing that very thing only shows how far from Christ the religious teachers of the day have gone. It is time that they and all men should be told that the law of God is the one perfect rule of human duty; that the Lord Jesus Christ is the one perfect example that has been worked out in this world under that rule; and that all men who will correctly solve the problem of human destiny must solve it by the terms of that rule as exemplified in, and according to, that example. Whoever attempts to solve the problem by any other rule or according to any other example will utterly fail of a correct solution; and whoever teaches men to attempt to solve it by any other rule or according to any other example, even though it be by "the example of the apostles," he both acts and teaches treason against the Lord Jesus Christ.

What, then, is the example of Christ in regard to keeping the first day of the week? There is no example about it at all. He never kept it. No one ever can—in fact no one ever does—claim any example of Christ for keeping the first day of the week. But where there is no example of Christ there *can* be no example of the apostles. Therefore there is not, and cannot be, any such thing as the example of the apostles for keeping the first day of the week.

What, then, is the example of Christ in regard to keeping the seventh day? He kept the first seventh day the world ever saw, when he had finished his great work of creation. When he came into the world, everybody knows that he kept it as long as he lived in the world. And "he that saith he abideth in him ought himself also so to walk even as he walked." Therefore those who walk as he walked will have to keep the seventh day. His steps led him to the place of worship on the seventh day, for thus "his custom was" (Luke 4:16), and he taught the people how to keep the seventh day, the Sabbath of the Lord (Matt. 12: 1-12). And he has left "us an example that ye should follow his steps." And all who follow his steps will be led by those steps to keep the seventh day, and to turn away their feet from the Sabbath, for such is his example.

Paul said, "Be ye followers of me, even as I also am of Christ." Now was Paul a follower of Christ in the matter of the seventh day? Let us see: "And he [Christ] came to Nazareth, where he had been brought up; and, *as his custom was*, he went into the synagogue on the Sabbath day, and *stood up for to read*." Luke 4:16. And of Paul it is said, by the same writer, "They came to Thessalonica, where was a synagogue of the Jews, and Paul, *as his manner* [*custom*] *was*, went in unto them, and three Sabbath days *reasoned with them out of the Scriptures*." Acts 17:1, 2. Paul *did* follow Christ in his "custom" of keeping the Sabbath day—the seventh day—therefore if any man will obey the word of God by Paul, and will be a follower of Paul as he followed Christ, it will have to be his "custom" to go to the house of God, and to worship God, on the seventh day.

For the keeping of the seventh day we have the commandment of God, the example of the living God (Ex. 20: 8–11; Gen. 2:3), and the example of the Lord Jesus Christ both in Heaven and on earth, both as Creator and Redeemer. And there is neither command nor example for the keeping of any other day. Will you obey the commandment of God, and follow the divine example in divine things? or will you instead obey a human command and follow human examples in human things, and expect the divine reward for it? Answer yourself now as you expect to answer God in the Judgment.

1 CORINTHIANS 16 : 2.

The next reference noticed by Mr. Elliott is 1 Cor. 16:1, 2, of which he writes—

"Another incidental allusion to the religious use of the day—an allusion none the less valuable because incidental—is the direction of Paul in 1 Cor. 16:1, 2: 'Now concerning the collection for the saints, as I have given order to the churches of Galatia, even so do ye. Upon the first day of the week let every one of you lay by him in store as God hath prospered him, that there be no gatherings when I come.' . . . The Corinthians were on that day to deposit their alms in a common treasury."—*Pp. 195, 196.*

Paul's direction is, "Let every one of you lay by *him* in store;" Mr. Elliott says they were "to deposit their alms in a common treasury." Now can a man lay by him in store, and deposit in a common treasury, the same money at the same time? If there are any, especially of those who keep Sunday, who think that it can be done, let them try it. Next Sunday, before you go to meeting find out how God has prospered you, and set apart accordingly that sum of money which you will lay by you in store by depositing it in the common treasury of the church. Then as you go to church, take the money along, and when the collection box is passed, put in it that which you are going to lay by you in store; and the work is done! According to Mr. Elliott's idea, you have obeyed this scripture. That is you have obeyed it by *putting away* from you the money which the Scripture directs you to *lay by* you. You have put into the hands of *others* that which is to be laid by *you*. You have *carried away* and placed entirely *beyond your control*, and where you will never see it again, that which is to be laid by you *in store*. In other words you have obeyed the Scripture by directly disobeying it.

True, that is a novel kind of obedience; but no one need be surprised at it in this connection; for that is the only kind of obedience to the Scripture that can ever be shown by keeping Sunday as the Sabbath. The commandment of God says "Remember the Sabbath day to keep it holy. . . . The seventh day is the Sabbath." And people propose to obey that commandment by remembering the first day instead of the seventh. The word of God says: "The seventh day is the Sabbath of the Lord thy God, *in it thou shalt not do any work*;" and people who keep Sunday propose to obey that word by working all day on the day in which God says they shall do no work. And so it is in perfect accord with the principles of the Sunday-sabbath that Mr. Elliott should convey the idea that 1 Cor. 16:2 was obeyed by doing directly the opposite of what the text says.

But he seeks to justify his theory by the following remark:—

"That this laying in store did not mean a simple hoarding of gifts by each one in his own house, is emphatically shown by the reason alleged for the injunction, 'that there be no gatherings' (*i. e.* "collections," the same word used in the first verse) 'when I come.' . . . If the gifts had had to be collected from house to house, the very object of the apostle's direction would have failed to be secured."

This reasoning might be well enough if it were true. But it is not true. This we know because Paul himself has told us just what he meant, and has shown us just what the Corinthians understood him to mean; and Mr. Elliott's theory is the reverse of Paul's record of facts. A year after writing the first letter to the Corinthians, Paul wrote the second letter; and in the second letter he makes explicit mention of this very "collection for the saints," about which he had given these directions in the first letter. In the second letter (chap. 9:1-5), Paul writes:—

"For as touching the ministering to the saints, it is superfluous for me to write to you; for I know the forwardness of your mind, for which I boast of you to them of Macedonia, that Achaia was ready a year ago; and your zeal hath provoked very many. *Yet have I sent the brethren,* lest our boasting of you should be in vain in this behalf; *that,* as I said, *ye may be ready;* lest haply if they of Macedonia come with me, *and find you unprepared,* we (that we say not, ye) should be ashamed in this same confident boasting. Therefore I thought it *necessary* to exhort the brethren, that they would go before unto you, *and make up beforehand your bounty,* whereof ye had notice before, *that the same might be* ready, as a matter of bounty, and not as of covetousness."

Now if Mr. Elliott's theory be correct, that the Corinthians were to deposit their alms in a common treasury each first day of the week, and if that was what Paul meant that they should do, then why should Paul think it "necessary" to send brethren before himself "to make up" this bounty, so "that it might be ready" when he came? If Mr. Elliott's theory be correct, what possible danger could there have been of these brethren finding the Corinthians "unprepared"? and why should Paul be afraid that they were unprepared? No; Mr. Elliott's theory and argument are contrary to the facts. In the first letter to the Corinthians (16:2), Paul meant just what he said, that on the first day of the week every one should "lay by him in store;" and the Corinthian Christians so understood it, and so likewise would everyone else understand it, were it not that its *perversion* is so sorely essential in bolstering up the baseless fabric of the Sunday Lord's day. But the Corinthians, having no such thing to cripple or pervert their ability to understand plain language, understood it as it was written, and as Paul meant that it should be understood. Each one laid by him as directed; then when the time came for Paul to go by them and take their alms to Jerusalem, he sent brethren before to make up the bounty which had been laid by in store, so that it might be ready when he came. Therefore, 1 Cor. 16:2 gives no sanction whatever to the idea of meetings on the first day of the week.

And now after all his peregrinations in search of the origin of the first day of the week as the Lord's day, Mr. Elliott arrives at the following intensely logical deduction:—

"The selection of the Lord's day by the apostles as the one festival day of the new society seems so obviously natural, and even necessary, that when we join to these considerations the fact that it was so employed, we can no longer deny to the religious use of Sunday the high sanction of apostolic authority."—*P. 198*.

All that we shall say to that is, that it is the best illustration that we have ever seen of the following rule, by "Rev. Levi Philetus Dobbs, D. D.,"—Dr. Wayland, editor of the *National Baptist*—for proving something when there is nothing with which to prove it. In fact we hardly expected ever to find in "real life" an illustration of the rule; but Mr. Elliott's five-hundred-dollar-prize logic has furnished a perfect illustration of it. The rule is:—

"Prove the premise by the conclusion, and then prove the conclusion by the premise; proving A by B and then proving B by A. And if the people believe the conclusion already (or think they do, which amounts to the same thing), and if you bring in now and then the favorite words and phrases that the people all want to hear, and that they have associated with orthodoxy, 'tis wonderful what a reputation you will get as a logician."

If "Dr. Dobbs" had offered a five-hundred-dollar prize for the best real example that should be worked out under that rule, we should give a unanimous, rising, rousing vote in favor of Rev. George Elliott and his "Abiding Sabbath" as the most deserving of the prize.

Yet with all this he finds "complete silence of the New Testament so far as any explicit command for the [Sunday] Sabbath or definite rules for its observance are concerned." What! A New Testament institution, and yet in the New Testament there is neither command nor rules for its observance!! Then how can it be possible that there can ever rest upon anybody any obligation whatever to observe it? How would it be possible anyhow to *observe* it without any rules for its observance? We shall now notice how he accounts for such an anomaly.

CHAPTER VIII.

THE COMMANDMENT FOR SUNDAY-KEEPING.

ALTHOUGH the author of "The Abiding Sabbath" finds complete silence in the New Testament in regard to any commands or rules for observance of the first day of the week, yet he insists that the Sunday-sabbath "is established as an apostolic institution;" and that "the religious use of Sunday" has "the high sanction of apostolic authority;" not only by the *example* of the apostles, but by their plain commands—in fact by commands so plain that they cannot be misunderstood. Thus he says:—

"Preachers of the gospel of the resurrection and founders of the church of the resurrection, they [the apostles] gave a new, sacred character to the day of the resurrection by their own example and by their *explicit injunctions.*"—*P. 198.*

Now an "injunction" is, "That which is enjoined; an order; *a command; a precept.*" Enjoin, is "to lay upon, as an order or command; *to give a command to; to direct with authority;*" "this word has the force of *pressing admonition.* It has also the sense of command." "'Explicit' denotes something which is set forth in the *plainest language,* so that it cannot be misunderstood."—*Webster.* "Explicit injunctions," then, are commands that are set forth in language so plain that they cannot be misunderstood. Therefore Mr. Elliott's unqualified declaration is that, by commands so plain that they cannot be misunderstood, the apostles have given a sacred character to Sunday. But everybody who ever read the New Testament knows that that is not true. *And so does Mr. Elliott*; for as already quoted, on page 184 he plainly confesses "the *complete silence* of the New Testament so far as any explicit command for the Sabbath or definite rules for its observance are concerned." And that by the word "Sabbath" in this place he means the Sunday is undoubted, because he immediately begins an argument to account for this "complete silence," and to justify it. But knowing and confessing as he does, "the *complete silence* of the New Testament so far as any *explicit command*" for the observance of the first day of the week is concerned, it is impossible to conceive by what mental process consistent with honesty, he could bring himself, in less than fifteen pages from these very words, to say that the apostles gave a "sacred character to the day of the resurrection by their own example and by their *explicit injunctions.*" Compare pages 184 and 198.

And it is by such proofs as this that Sunday is shown to be the Lord's day and the Christian Sabbath! It is such stuff as this that Professor William Thompson, D. D., Professor Llewellyn Pratt, D. D., and Rev. George M. Stone, D. D., all of Hartford, Conn., "after a *careful*(?) and *thorough*(?!) examination" accounted worthy of a prize of five hundred dollars; and to which, by a copyright, the American Tract Society has set its seal of orthodoxy; and which the Woman's Christian Temperance Union names as one of the books on the Sabbath question which "at least" "should be put into every district, Sunday-school, and other public library."

But although he finds this "complete silence," he finds no difficulty in accounting for it; and here is how he does it:—

It is not difficult to account for the complete silence of the New Testament so far as any explicit command for the Sabbath or definite rules for its observance are concerned. . . . *The conditions under which the early Christian church existed were not favorable for their announcement.* . . . The early church, a struggling minority composed of the poorest people, *could not* have instituted the Christian Sabbath in its full force of meaning. The ruling influences of government and society were against them.—*P. 184.*

Therefore, according to this five-hundred-dollar-prize Christianity, commandments for the observance of Christian duties can be announced only when the conditions under which the church exists are favorable to their announcement; that is, when the ruling influences of government and society are in favor of it. And the one great distinguishing institution of Christianity is dependent upon "the ruling influences of government and society," for "its full force and meaning"! Christians can wear the badge of their profession only when the majority favor it! We confess that that is in fact the true doctrine of the Sunday-sabbath. We have heard it preached often. And we know that is the doctrine upon which it was based in the origin of its claim to Christian recognition. But is that the kind of religion that Christ instituted in the world? Is that the manner of "Christian walk and conversation" to which he referred when he said: "Enter ye in [strive to enter in] at the strait gate; for wide is the gate, and broad is the way, that leadeth to destruction, and *many* there be which go in thereat; because strait is the gate, and narrow is the way, which leadeth unto life, and *few* there be that find it"? Was it to incite his disciples to faithfulness under the favor of "the ruling influences of government and society" that Christ said, "The brother shall deliver up the brother to death, and the father the child; the children shall rise up against their parents, and cause them to be put to death. And ye shall be hated of all men for my name's sake; but he that endureth to the end shall be saved"? Was it to induce the "early Christian church" to wait for the sanction of the majority, and the favor of "the ruling influences of government and society," that Christ gave the command, "What I tell you in darkness, that speak ye in light; and what ye hear in the ear, that preach ye upon the house-tops. And fear not them which kill the body, but are not able to kill the soul; but rather fear him which is able to destroy both soul and body in hell"? The fact is that Mr. Elliott's reason for the "complete silence" of the New Testament in regard to a command for the observance of the Sunday, as well as the doctrine of the Sunday-sabbath itself, is contrary to every principle of the doctrine of Christ.

But according to Mr. Elliott's scheme of Christian duty and faithfulness, when was the "Christian Sabbath" really instituted "in its full force of meaning"? He tells us plainly. Hear him:—

"For the perfect establishment of the Christian Sabbath, as has already been observed, there was needed a social revolution in the Roman Empire. *The infant church*, in its struggles through persecution and martyrdom, *had not the power even to keep the Lord's day perfectly* itself, much less could the sanctity of the day be guarded from desecration by unbelievers. We should expect therefore to find the institution making a deepening groove on society and in history, and becoming a well-defined ordinance the very moment that Christianity became a dominant power. That such was the case the facts fully confirm. From the records of the early church and the works of the Christian Fathers we can clearly see the growth of the institution culminating in *the famous edict of Constantine*, when Christianity became the established religion of the empire."—*P. 213.*

Now as there was no command for the observance of the Sunday institution, and as it was not, and could not be, kept by the "struggling minority" that formed the early Christian church, the "deepening groove on society and in history" that was made by "the institution," could have been made only by influences from beyond the struggling minority, *i. e.*, from the majority. And that is the fact. The majority were heathen.

The worship of the sun was the chief worship of all the heathen. And as ambitious bishops, in their lust of power, of numbers, and "of the ruling influences of government and society," opened the way for the heathen to come into the church, bringing with them their heathen practices and customs, the *day of the sun*, being the chief of these, thus gained a place under the name of Christianity, and so went on making its "deepening groove on society and in history," until it culminated in "the famous edict of Constantine," in honor of "the venerable day of the sun," and commanding its partial observance. Of this famous edict, we shall let the author of the "Abiding Sabbath" himself tell:—

"The Emperor Constantine was converted, and Christianity became, practically, the religion of the empire. *It was now possible to enforce the Christian Sabbath and make its observance universal.* In the year 321, consequently, was issued the famous edict of Constantine commanding abstinence from servile labor on Sunday. The following is the full text:—

"'THE EMPEROR CONSTANTINE TO HELPIDIUS.

"'On the venerable day of the sun, let the magistrates and people living in towns rest, and let all workshops be closed. Nevertheless, in the country, those engaged in the cultivation of land may freely and lawfully work, because it often happens that another day is not so well fitted for sowing grain and planting vines; lest by neglect of the best time, the bounty provided by Heaven should be lost. Given the seventh day of March, Crispus and Constantine being consuls, both for the second time.'"—*P. 228.*

The man who can see in the life of Constantine any evidences of conversion, possesses a degree of penetration truly wonderful; equal, indeed to that which can discern "transient elements" where it demonstrates that there are none. The one act of Constantine which is most nearly consistent with the idea of conversion, was performed in March, A. D. 313, eight years before the earliest date we have ever heard claimed for his conversion. That act was the edict of Milan, "the great act of toleration," which "confirmed to each individual of the Roman world the privilege of choosing and professing his own religion," and stopped the persecution of Christians. But even this one act that was consistent with conversion, was undone by his "conversion," for soon after his "conversion" the edict of Milan was revoked. We shall name here some of his principal acts after his "conversion:" March 7, A. D. 321, he issued an edict in honor of the venerable day of the sun. The very next day, March 8, 321, he issued an edict commanding the consultation of the soothsayers. In 323 Licinius was murdered by his orders, in violation of a solemn oath given to his own sister, Constantia. In 325 he convoked, and presided at, the Council of Nice. In 326 he was guilty of the murder of his own son, Crispus, his nephew, Licinius, and his wife, Fausta, to say nothing of others. In 328 he laid the foundation of Constantinople according to "the ancient ritual of Roman Paganism," and in 330 the city was dedicated to the Virgin Mary. Afterward he set up in the same city the images of the deities of Paganism—Minerva, Cybele, Amphitrite, Pan, and the Delphic Tripod of the oracle of Apollo—"and of all the statues which were introduced from different quarters none were received with greater honor than those of Apollo." But above all, as though he would give to the whole world the most abiding proof of his Paganism, he erected a pillar, over a hundred and twenty feet high, and on the top of it he placed an image in which he "dared to mingle together the attributes of the Sun of Christ, and of himself."—*Milman, History of Christianity, book 3, chap. 3, par. 7*

To the end of his life he continued to imprint the *image* of Apollo on one side of his imperial coins, and the *name* of Christ on the other. In view of these things it may be safely and sincerely doubted whether he was ever converted at all. And we most decidedly call in question the Christian principle that could dwell consistently with a life so largely made up of heathen practices, and stained with so much blood.

But to say nothing further on the subject of the "conversion" of Constantine, it is evident from Mr. Elliott's argument that the "influences of government and society which were essential to the complete sanctity of the "Christian Sabbath," and for which it was compelled to wait nearly three hundred years, were embodied in an imperial edict of such a man, in honor —not of the Lord's day, nor of the Christian Sabbath, nor of Christ, but—of the venerable day of the sun; that the legislation which was to enforce the "Christian Sabbath," and make its observance universal, was a piece of legislation that enforced the "venerable day of the sun," and made its observance partial, that is, obligatory upon *only* the *people who lived in towns*, and such as *worked at trades;* while country people might "freely and *lawfully* work." However, on the nature of this legislation, we need ourselves to make no further comment. The author of "The Abiding Sabbath" exposes it so completely that we can better let him do it here. He says:—

"To fully understand the provisions of this legislation, the peculiar position of Constantine must be taken into consideration. He was not himself free from all remains of heathen superstition. It seems certain that before his conversion he had been particularly devoted to the worship of Apollo, the sun-god. . . . The problem before him was to legislate for the new faith in such a manner as *not to seem entirely inconsistent with his old practices,* and *not to* come in *conflict with the prejudices of his pagan subjects.* These facts serve to explain the peculiarities of this decree. He names the holy day, not the Lord's day, but the 'day of the sun,' *the heathen designation,* and thus at once seems *to identify it with his former Apollo-worship;* he excepts the country from the operation of the law, and thus avoids collision with his heathen subjects."—*P. 229.*

Now as he had been particularly devoted to the worship of Apollo, the sun-god; as he shaped this edict so as not to be inconsistent with his old practices, and not to conflict with the prejudices of his pagan subjects; as he gives the day its heathen designation, and thus identifies it with his former Apollo-worship; and as in it he avoids collision with his heathen subjects; then we should like to know where in the edict there comes in any legislation for his *Christian* subjects. In other words, if he had intended to legislate solely and entirely for his heathen subjects, and to enjoin a heathen practice, could he have framed an edict that would more clearly show it than does the one before us? Impossible. Therefore, by Mr. Elliott's own comments, it is demonstrated that the famous edict of Constantine was given wholly in favor of the heathen, enjoining the observance of a heathen institution, Sunday, in honor of the great heathen god, the sun. And if *that* was to favor Christianity, then so much the worse for the Christianity(?) which it favored. At the very best it could only be heathenism under the name of Christianity. And in fact that is all it was.

Such is the command, and such its source, that it is seriously proposed shall be observed instead of the holy commandment of the living God, spoken with a voice that shook the earth, and twice written with his own blazing finger upon the enduring stone. Such is the day, and such its sanctions, that it is proposed shall wholly supplant the day to which have been given "the highest and strongest sanctions possible even to Deity,"—the day upon which God rested, which he blessed, which he sanctified, and which he has distinctly commanded us to keep, saying, "Remember the Sabbath day, to keep it holy." "*The seventh day* is the Sabbath of the Lord thy God; in it thou shalt not do any work." The observance of the seventh day is that which we, by the word of God, urge upon the conscience of every man. But if we had no better reasons for it than are given in this five-hundred-dollar-prize essay, or than we have ever seen given, for the observance of Sunday, we should actually be ashamed ever to put our pen to paper to advocate it.

CHAPTER IX.

THE FATHERS, ETC.

As WE have shown, the author of the "Abiding Sabbath" fills up, with the heathen edict of Constantine for the partial observance of Sunday, the blank left by "the complete silence of the New Testament" so far as any command or rules on that subject are concerned; yet his system is not complete without the sanction of the Fathers. So, as is the custom of the advocates of Sunday observance, he gives to the Fathers, the Councils, the popes, and the Catholic saints, a large place in his five-hundred-dollar-prize argument for Sunday keeping. We have before cited one of the rules laid down by the Rev. Levi Philetus Dobbs, D. D., for proving a thing when there is nothing with which to prove it, and have given an example from the "Abiding Sabbath" in illustration of the rule. We here present another of the Doctor's rules, and in Mr. Elliott's treatment of the Fathers, our readers can see its application. Says Dr. Dobbs:—

"I regard, however, a judicious use of the Fathers as being, on the whole, the best reliance for anyone who is in the situation of my querist. The advantages of the Fathers are twofold: first, they carry a good deal of weight with the masses; and secondly, you can find whatever you want in the Fathers. I don't believe that any opinion could be advanced so foolish, so manifestly absurd, but that you can find passages to sustain it, on the pages of these venerable stagers. And to the common mind, one of these is just as good as another. If it happens that the point you want to prove is one that never chanced to occur to the Fathers, why, you can easily show that they would have taken your side if they had only thought of the matter. And if, perchance, there is nothing bearing even remotely or constructively on the point, don't be discouraged; get a good strong quotation and put the name of the Fathers to it, and utter it with an air of triumph; it will be all just as well; nine-tenths of the people don't stop to ask whether a quotation bears on the matter in hand. Yes, my brother, the Fathers are your stronghold. They are Heaven's best gift to *the man who has a cause that can't be sustained in any other way.*" (See Appendix.)

The first of the Fathers to whom Mr. Elliott refers is Clement of Rome, who he says died about A. D. 100. From Clement he quotes a passage which says nothing about any particular day, much less does it say that Sunday is the Lord's day, or the "abiding Sabbath," and of it the author of the "Abiding Sabbath" says:—

"This passage does not indeed refer by name to the Lord's day, but it proves conclusively the existence at that time of prescribed seasons of worship, and asserts their appointment by the Saviour himself."—*P. 214.*

But for all it mentions no day, it is, says he, an "important link in the argument" that proves that Sunday is the Lord's day and of "perpetual obligation." An argument in which such a thing as that is counted "an important link," must be sorely pushed to find a connection that will hold it up.

His next link is no better. This time he proposes a quotation from Ignatius, and of it says:—

"The passage is obscure, and the text doubtless corrupt, but the trend of meaning is not indistinct." —*P. 215, note.*

It seems to us that an institution that has to be supported by an argument that is dependent upon a "trend of meaning," drawn from an "obscure passage," in a "corrupt text," is certainly of most questionable authority. True, he says "the argument can do without it if necessary;" but it is particularly to be noticed that *his* argument does not do without it, and he deems it of sufficient importance to devote more than a page of his book to its consideration. We would remark, also, that we have never yet seen nor heard an extended argument for the Sunday institution that did do without it.

His next quotation is from a writing of about equal value with this of Ignatius. He says:—

"Here may be introduced a quotation from the so-called Epistle of Barnabas. . . . The external evidence of the authorship of this writing would be convincing but for the discredit which its internal characters casts upon it."—*Pp. 216, 217, note.*

That is to say, we might consider this epistle genuine if the writing itself did not show the contrary. And as if to make as strong as possible the doubt of its genuineness, he adds:—

"There is a very close relationship between this writing and the 'Teaching of the Twelve Apostles.'"

And to the "Teaching" he refers by the doubting phrase, "if genuine." Well let us see what this "Teaching" is worth. We need not go outside of the document itself to successfully impeach its credit in the estimation of all people who have any regard for the rights of property. We here make the distinct charge that the document entitled "The Teaching of the Apostles," *plainly teaches that it is right to steal.* Proof: in Chapter I we find these words: "If one that is in need taketh, *he shall be guiltless.*" And to show that it is theft that is meant, we have but to read right on: "But he that is *not in need* shall give account whereof he *took* and whereunto; and *being in durance* [imprisonment] shall be questioned touching what he did, and he shall not go out thence until he give back the last farthing."

According to this precious document then all that is requisite is to be "in need," and then if he "taketh, he shall be guiltless." A man is surely in need of a suit of clothes; he "taketh" one and "shall be guiltless." Another is in need of a horse; he "taketh," and "shall be guiltless." Another is in great need of bread; he "taketh" a sack of flour, and "shall be guiltless;" and so on to the end of the catalogue. How the socialists, the communists, the nihilists, and the anarchists generally, may be glad and shout for joy, and fling their ready caps in air at sight of "The Teaching of the Apostles," this wondrous screed, this last, best gift to the rascals!

Well may Mr. Elliott attack to this document the saving clause "if genuine." But why should he want to receive and use it, as he does, even with that qualification? Does he not know that such is not the genuine teaching of the apostles? Oh, yes, of course he does, but in this precious document there is a phrase that can be made to do duty in support of Sunday as the Lord's day, and that blessed consideration sanctifies all else, even to its tenets sanctioning theft. And between "the so-called Epistle of Barnabas" and this document "there is a very close relationship"! We do not doubt it in the least. But there is no relationship at all between either of these productions and the genuine teaching of the apostles. No, such is *not* the teaching of the apostles of Christ; but it shows how very degenerate the Christianity of the day has become, when it receives so gladly, and extols so highly, as the veritable teaching of the Spirit of God, a production that is a shame to man.

Then after mention of Pliny's letter to Trajan, Justin Martyr, Melito, the "Teaching," and Irenæus, he comes to Clement of Alexandria, of whom he speaks as follows:—

"Clement of Alexandria, A. D. 194, in a mystical exposition of the fourth commandment, in the midst of fanciful speculations on the religious signification of numbers, comes down long enough from the loftier flights of his spiritual arithmetic to tell us that the seventh day of the law has given place to the eighth day of the gospel. . . *Nobody*, of course, *can tell what far-fetched and unheard-of meanings* may lie underneath the words of the good semi-Gnostic Father; but as far as his testimony goes, it *helps* to establish the fact that the first day of the week filled the same place in the minds of the church of that time, that the seventh day had occupied in the Jewish system."—*P. 223*.

Certainly. It matters not what "mystical expositions," nor what "fanciful interpretations," nor what "far-fetched and unheard-of meanings" there may be, they all "help to establish" the heathen institution of Sunday, in the place of the day made holy and commanded to be kept so, by the Creator of the heavens and the earth.

With just one more witness he closes the second century. And it is most fittingly done, as follows:—

"This century will be concluded with the mention of *that most brilliant and erratic of all* the ante-Nicene Christian writers, Tertullian, of Carthage. . . This *vehement writer* fitly closes this list of evidences of the honored place filled by the Lord's day in the first two centuries of the Christian church."—*Pp. 223, 224*.

Fitly, indeed, does this "vehement writer," and most erratic of all the ante-Nicene Fathers, close the list of the first two centuries. But what a list! He gives us a list of ten witnesses to prove that Sunday is the Lord's day, and that it was observed as such in the first two centuries, and by his own words it is shown that the first one does not mention the day at all; the second is an obscure passage in a corrupt text; the third is doubtful; the fourth speaks only of a "stated day," without giving it any title at all; the fifth "calls it by its heathen name;" the seventh is doubtful but teaches that men may steal if they are in need; the ninth is so mystical, so fanciful, that "nobody can tell what far-fetched and unheard-of meanings may lie underneath his words;" the tenth is the "most brilliant and erratic [having no certain course; roaming about without a fixed destination] of all," and this "vehement ["furious; violent; impetuous; passionate; ardent; hot"] writer,"—we do not wonder that Dean Milman calls him "this fiery African"—*this* witness "fitly closes the list of evidences of the honored place filled by the Lord's day in the first two centuries!" Well we should say so. But what is a point worth that is "proved" by such evidences? It is worth all that the Sunday-sabbath is, which is supported by it, and that is—nothing. Yet these are the only witnesses that can be called, and false, doubtful, and untrustworthy though they be, they must be used or the Sunday institution will fail. But whether the failure would be any greater without such proofs than with them, we leave the reader to decide. And that is part of the argument for the obligation of Sunday, that was accounted worth a prize of five hundred dollars! We should like very much to see an argument on that question which that committee of award would consider to be worth nothing.

After this array of five-hundred-dollar-prize witnesses for Sunday, we hope our readers will justify us in declining to follow Mr. Elliott through a further list, composed of Origen, and Athanasius, Theodosius the Great, and Emperor Leo the Thracian, and a number of Catholic saints, such as Hilary, Ambrose, Augustine, "Chrysostom the golden-mouthed," and Jerome, " the foul-mouthed " *(Mosheim, Cent. 4, part 2, chap. 2, last par. but one)*; through the Councils of Nice, Sardica, Gangra, Antioch, First of Toledo, Fourth of Carthage, and that of Laodicæa, and so on down to the Synod of Dort, and the Westminster Assembly.

Yet his work on this division of his subject would be incomplete, and out of harmony with his method of argument throughout, if he should not turn about and upset it all. Accordingly, therefore, he at once destroys the edifice which he has thus so laboriously erected. Among the dangers which threaten the Sunday institution of to-day he declares that:—

"Dangerous is the substitution of the dictum of the church for the warrant of Holy Scripture. . . To make the Lord's day only an ecclesiastical contrivance, is to give no assurance to the moral reason, and to lay no obligation upon a free conscience. *The church cannot maintain this institution by its own edict.* Council, assembly, convocation, and synod can impose a law on the conscience *only* when they are able to back their decree *with* ' *Thus saith the Lord.*' "—*P. 263.*

The only dictum that the author of "The Abiding Sabbath" has shown for the Sunday-sabbath is the dictum of the church. The only means by which he has fixed the day to be observed is "by a religious *consensus* of the Christian church" (*P. 203*). The only edicts which he had presented are the heathen edicts of Constantine, additional laws by Constantine and Theodosius the Great, and the decree of Emperor Leo the Thracian. It is only in these, and the action of council, assembly, convocation, and synod that he obtains authority to impose the observance of Sunday as a law upon the conscience. He has given no "Thus saith the Lord" for the institution nor for its observance; but on the contrary has confessed the "complete silence of the New Testament," in regard to any command or rules for either the institution or its observance. Therefore, by his own argument, the observance of Sunday as the Sabbath is of "no obligation upon a free conscience." And that is the truth.

CHAPTER X.

"THE CHANGE OF DAY."

UNDER the title of "The Change of Day," the author of "The Abiding Sabbath" devotes a chapter to the denial of the right of the seventh day to be considered the Sabbath; and he starts with the attempt to make a distinction between the Sabbath as an institution, and the Sabbath as the name of a day. He says:—

"Let it be urged that the Sabbath as an institution, and the Sabbath as the name of a day, are entirely distinct."—*P. 201.*

This is a turn that is quite commonly taken by those who deny that the seventh day is the Sabbath, but we wish that some of those who think they see this distinction, would describe what they call the "institution." We wish they would tell us what it is. We wish they would tell us how the "institution" was made, and how it can be observed distinct from the day. For says Mr. Elliott:—

"The particular day is no essential part of the institution."—*P. 203.*

If, therefore, the day be no essential part of the institution, it follows that the institution can be observed without reference to the day; and so we say we should like for Mr. Elliott, or someone else who thinks the proposition correct, to tell us how that can be done. But Mr. Elliott does not believe the proposition, nor does anyone else whom we have ever known to state it. In his argument under this very proposition that, "The particular day is no essential part of the institution," Mr. Elliott says:—

"Without doubt, the spiritual intent of the Sabbath will fail of full realization *except all men unite upon one day.*"—*Id.*

Then what his argument amounts to is just this: The particular day is no essential part of the institution, yet the institution will fail of proper realization unless all unite upon a particular day. In other words, the particular day *is* an essential part of the institution. And that is exactly where everyone lands who starts with this proposition. But it is not enough to say that the day is an essential *part* of the institution. The day *is* the institution, and the institution is the day. And if the particular day be taken away, the institution is destroyed. The commandment of God is not, Remember the Sabbath *institution*, to keep it holy. Nor is it merely, Remember the Sabbath, as though it were something indefinite. But it is plainly, "Remember the Sabbath *day*, to keep it holy." Ex. 20 : 8. The word of God is not that he blessed the Sabbath *institution*, and hallowed it. But the word is, "The Lord blessed the Sabbath *day*, and hallowed *it.*" Ex. 20 : 11.

Nor is it left to men to select, and unite upon, some

"one day" to be the Sabbath. The Lord not only commands men to remember the Sabbath day, to keep it holy, but he also tells them, as plainly as language can tell, that "the *seventh day* is the Sabbath." It is the seventh day that God blessed at creation. It is the seventh day that he then sanctified. It is the seventh day upon which he rested. Gen. 2:2, 3. It was the rest, the blessing, and the sanctification of the seventh day that made the institution of the Sabbath. And it is simply the record of a fact, when the Lord wrote on the table of stone, "The seventh day is the Sabbath." Suppose the question should be asked, What is the Sabbath? As the word of God is true, the only true answer that can be given is, "*The seventh day* is the Sabbath." Therefore it is as plain as words can make it, that apart from the seventh day there is no Sabbath; and that apart from the seventh day there is no Sabbath institution.

Again, the word Sabbath means *rest*, and with this Mr. Elliott agrees; he says:—

"The word 'Sabbath' is the one used in the fourth commandment; it means 'rest,' and it is the substantive form of the verb employed in Gen. 2:2, 3, also Ex. 31:17, to describe the divine resting after creation."—*P. 202.*

But God did not bless the *rest*, he blessed the rest *day;* he did not hallow the *rest*, he hallowed the rest *day*. That rest day was the seventh day, the last day of the week. "And he rested on the seventh day from all his work which he had made. And God blessed *the seventh day* and sanctified *it;* because that in it he had rested from all his work which God created and made." Did God rest any day of the week but the seventh day? Assuredly not. Then is not the seventh day the rest day of God? Most certainly. Then whenever anybody calls any day the Sabbath but the seventh day—the last day of the week—he not only contradicts the plain word of God but he also contradicts the very language in which he himself speaks, because he gives the title of "rest" to that which by no possibility can truthfully bear it. The word of God is the truth, and it says, "The seventh day is the Sabbath [rest] of the Lord thy God; in it thou shalt not do any work."

Yet in the face of his own reference to Gen. 2:2, 3, and Ex. 31:17, the author of the "Abiding Sabbath" has the assurance to write the following:—

"As a human monument the particular day has value, but it has no bearing on that divine ordinance of rest and worship which comes to us out of eternity and blends again with it at the end of time."—*P. 203.*

"As a *human* monument?" How did the particular day—the seventh day—in Gen. 2:2, 3 become a human monument? What human being had anything to do with the erection of that monument? It was God who set up that monument, and when an institution established by the Lord himself, can be called a human monument, we should like to know how much further a five-hundred-dollar prize would not justify a man in going.

And again, "The particular day has no bearing upon that divine ordinance which comes to us out of eternity." This, too, when the particular day *is* that divine ordinance. If the particular day has no bearing upon that divine ordinance of *rest* and worship which comes to us out of eternity, then what is the ordinance, and how can it be observed? This brings him again to the important concession that, "all men must unite upon one day," or else the Sabbath will fail of its proper realization. But we would ask, Did not the Lord know that when he made the Sabbath? Did he not know that it is necessary that all men should unite upon one day? We are certain that he did, and that he made ample provision for it. He himself selected the day which should be the Sabbath. He rested a certain definite day, he blessed that day, and he set it apart from the other days of the week, and he commanded man—the human race—to remember that day, and to do no work therein. That day is the last day of the week, the seventh day, and not the first day of the week. But the day which the Lord has chosen to be the Sabbath; the day which he has put honor upon; the day which he has by his own divine words and acts set apart from all other days; the day which he by his own voice from Heaven has commanded to be kept holy; that day which he has called his own—is to be set aside by men as not essential, and a heathen institution, by the authority of a heathen commandment, exalted to the place of the Lord's day, and as all-essential. But it is wickedness.

Like the majority of people who keep Sunday, the author of the "Abiding Sabbath" finds great difficulty in fixing the day, when the Sabbath of the Lord—the seventh day—is under discussion, but not the least difficulty when the first day of the week is to be pointed out. He inquires:—

"When does the day commence and end? Shall we define, as in the first chapter of Genesis, that the 'evening and morning' make a day, and therefore reckon from sunset to sunset, as did the Puritans? or shall we keep the civil day, from midnight to midnight?"—*P. 204.*

To those who regard the word of God as of any authority, we should think the day as defined in the first chapter of Genesis would be sufficient, and that therefore they would reckon the day as the Bible does, and as Mr. Elliott knows how to do, that is, "from sunset to sunset." But those who choose a heathen institution —Sunday—instead of the institution of God—the Sabbath day—we should expect to find reckoning as the heathen did, that is, "from midnight to midnight." And nothing more plainly marks the heathen origin of the Sunday institution, and the heathen authority for its observance, than does the fact that it is reckoned from midnight to midnight. If the religious observance of Sunday had been introduced by the apostles, or enjoined by any authority of God, it would have been observed and reckoned as the Bible gives the reckoning, from sunset to sunset. But instead of that, the Sunday institution bears Rome on its very face. Rome from her beginning reckoned the day from midnight to midnight. Sunday was the great heathen Roman day; and when by the working of the "mystery of iniquity," and Constantine's heathen edict, and his political, hypocritical conversion, this "wild solar holiday of all pagan times" was made the great papal Roman day, it was still essentially the same thing; and so it is yet. However much Protestants may dress it up, and call it the "Christian Sabbath," and the "Lord's day," the fact still remains that the Lord never called it his day; that there is nothing about it either Sabbatic or Christian, for the Lord never rested on it, and Christ never gave any direction whatever in regard to it; and that it rests essentially upon human authority, and *that* of heathen origin.

Now he says:—

"As a concession to that human weakness which is troubled after eighteen centuries' drill in spiritual religion, about the particular day of the week to be honored, the question will be fairly met."—*P. 205.*

Remember, he has promised that the question shall "be fairly met." And the proposition with which he starts in fulfillment of that promise, is this:—

"There is no possible means of fixing the day of the original Sabbath."—*Ib.*

Let us see. The Scripture says at the close of the six days employed in creation, that God "rested on the seventh day from all his work which he had made;" that he "blessed the seventh day and sanctified it; because that in it he had rested." Gen. 2:

2, 3. In the fourth commandment, God spake and wrote with direct reference to the day upon which he rested from creation, and pointed out that day as the one upon which the people should rest, saying: "The seventh day is the Sabbath of the Lord thy God; in it thou shalt not do any work. . . . For [because] in six days the Lord made heaven and earth, the sea, and all that in them is, and rested the seventh day; wherefore [for this reason] the Lord blessed the Sabbath day, and hallowed it." Therefore nothing can be plainer than that God, in the fourth commandment, pointed out distinctly "the day of the original Sabbath." The word of God says also that the day the Saviour lay in the grave certain persons "rested the Sabbath day *according to the commandment.*" Luke 23: 56. The Sabbath day according to the commandment, is the day of the original Sabbath. When those persons rested the Sabbath day according to the commandment, they rested the day of the original Sabbath. Therefore the day of the original Sabbath is fixed by the word of God to the day which followed the crucifixion of the Saviour. And that same word declares that the day which followed this day of the original Sabbath, was the first day of the week. Mr. Elliott finds no difficulty at all in fixing the first day of the week—the day of the resurrection of the Saviour. But the day of the original Sabbath is the day which immediately precedes the first day of the week. Therefore, as Mr. Elliott finds it not only possible but *easy* to fix the first day of the week, how can it be that he finds it impossible to fix the day of the original Sabbath, which immediately precedes the first day of the week?

But our author proceeds to *argue* the proposition, and this is how he begins :—

"Who can tell on what day of the week the first man was created?"—*Ib.*

Shall we grant Mr. Elliott's implied meaning, and conclude that he does not know on what day of the week the first man was created? Not at all; for within eight lines of this question, he begins to tell us of the day on which man first existed. He says:—

"For the sake, however, of any literalists who still believe that the work of creation began on Sunday eve, and ended Friday at sunset, it may be suggested that *the seventh day of creation was the first day of man's existence.*"

There, reader, you have it. He himself knows what day of the week the first man was created. For as "the seventh day of creation was man's first day of existence," it follows inevitably that man must have been created on the seventh day, unless indeed he supposes that man was created one day and did not exist till another! But who ever before heard of "the seventh day *of creation*"?! We cannot imagine where he ever learned of such a thing. Never from the Bible, certainly; for the Bible tells of only *six* days of creation. The first chapter of Genesis gives the record of the six days of creation; and in the fourth commandment God declares, "In *six days* the

Lord made heaven and earth, the sea, and *all that in them is.*" The Bible tells plainly that man was created on the sixth day. But lo, Mr. Elliott finds *seven* days of creation, and that the seventh day of creation was the first day of man's existence!! What a wonderful thing a five-hundred-dollar-prize essay is! It brings such large returns of nonsense for such a small investment of wisdom!

Well, what is Mr. Elliott's conclusion from this line of argument? Here it is:—

"If he [man] began the calculation of the week from that time, and kept the same Sabbath with his Maker, then the first day of the week, and not the seventh, was the primitive and patriarchal Sabbath. If a crude, bald literalism is to be the rule of interpretation, let us follow it boldly, no matter where it takes us."—*P. 206.*

We should say that if crude, bald nonsense is to characterize the argument by which the Sunday-sabbath is supported, then the essay entitled "The Abiding Sabbath" is fully entitled to the five-hundred-dollar prize which it received. This is the only reply that we shall make to this argument, for he himself knows that it is worthless; and he feels the necessity of making an apology for it, which he does, saying:—

"This suggestion is made, *not for any value which it possesses,* in itself, but as a fair illustration of the difficulties attending any attempt to fix the day."—*Ib.*

But is it "a *fair* illustration"? We are certain that it is not. And we are equally certain that if an honest inquiry were made for the day which *God has fixed* as the day of the original and only Sabbath of the Lord, it would, in every case, be found with less than a hundredth part of the difficulty that has attended this self-contradictory prize, or any other effort, to show that Sunday is the Sabbath.

But why talk about "the change of the Sabbath"? While creation stands, to change the Sabbath is impossible. And even though the present creation were swept away and a new one formed, even then it would be impossible to change the Sabbath to the first day of the week. Study this point a moment:—

Sabbath means rest. The Sabbath day is the rest day; and "God did rest the seventh day from all his works." Heb. 4:4. As, therefore, the seventh day is the day upon which God rested, that is the only day that can be the rest day. God rested no other day of the week, therefore no other day of the week can be the rest day. And so long as it remains the fact that "God did rest the seventh day from all his works," so long it will be the truth that the seventh day is the Sabbath. This discovers the utter absurdity of the idea that is so prevalent, and which is so much talked, and printed, and spread abroad, that "the Sabbath has been changed." To speak of a real change of the Sabbath, is but to say that the rest of God has been changed from the day upon which he rested to one upon which he did not rest. In other words, it is to say that the Lord rested upon a day upon which he did not rest. But that it is impossible for even the Lord to do, for to call that a *rest* day upon which he *worked* would not be the truth, and it is impossible for God to lie.

The seventh day, the Sabbath of the Lord, rests upon facts, and it is impossible to change facts. Fact is from *factum*—that which is done. When a thing has been done, it will remain a fact to all eternity. To all eternity it will remain the truth that it was done. It may be undone, yet the fact remains that it was done. No power in the universe can change a fact. It is a fact that in six days God created the heavens and the earth, and all things that are therein. This can never cease to be a fact. This earth might be relegated again to chaos, yet the fact would remain that in six days God did create it. It would likewise remain a fact that the Lord worked each of the six days. And as long as this world stands, which was created in these six days, so long will it remain impossible truthfully to call any one of these six days the Sabbath, that is, the rest day, because there stands the *fact* that the Lord worked, and, we repeat, he himself cannot call that a rest day in which he worked. It is likewise a fact that God did rest the seventh day. That can never cease to be the truth. Though the whole creation which God created should be blotted out, it would still remain the fact that God did rest the seventh day. And as long as the creation stands, so long the truth stands that the seventh day is the rest day, the Sabbath of the Creator; and that none other can be. Therefore it is the simple, plain, demonstrated truth that the seventh day of the week, and that day only of all in the week, is the Sabbath of the Lord; and that while creation stands it cannot be changed.

There is, however, a way, and only one conceivable way, in which the Sabbath could be changed; that is, as expressed by Alexander Campbell, *by creation being gone through with again.* Let us take Mr. Campbell's conception and suppose that creation is to be gone through with again for the purpose of changing the Sabbath; and suppose that the present creation is turned once more to chaos. In creating again, the Lord could of course employ as many, or as few, days as he pleased, according to the day which he designed to make the Sabbath. If he should employ nine days in the work of creation, and rest the tenth day, then the tenth day would be of course the Sabbath. Or, if he should employ eight days or seven days in creation and rest the ninth or the eighth, as the case might be, that day would be the Sabbath. Or he might employ five days in creation and rest the sixth, then the sixth day would be the Sabbath; or employ four days, and rest the *fifth;* or three days, and rest the *fourth;* or two days, and rest the *third;* or one day, and rest the *second.* Then the fifth, the fourth, the third, or the second day, as the case might be, would be the Sabbath.

But suppose it should be designed to make the first day the Sabbath. Could it be done? Not possibly. For suppose all things were created in one day, the day on which creation was performed would necessarily, and of itself, be the first day: therefore the rest day, the Sabbath, could not possibly be earlier than the second day. The first day could not possibly be both a working day and a rest day. It matters not though only a portion of the day should be employed in the *work*, it would effectually destroy the possibility of its being a rest day. So upon the hypothesis of a new creation, and upon that hypothesis alone, it is conceivable that the Sabbath could be changed; but even upon *that* hypothesis, it would be literally impossible to change the Sabbath from the seventh day to the *first day.*

People will talk and write glibly about the change of the Sabbath, never pausing to consider what is involved in the idea; never considering that heaven and earth would have to be removed before such a thing could be done. Even as Christ said, "It is easier for heaven and earth to pass, than one tittle of the law to fail." And, "Till heaven and earth pass, one jot or one tittle shall in nowise pass from the law." In the prophecy which foretold this attempt of "the man of sin" to change the Sabbath, the word is not that he should change the law, but that, "He shall *think* to change times and laws" of the Most High. This might be expected of the power that should oppose and exalt himself above God (2 Thess. 2: 3, 4); and it is perfectly in keeping with his character that in his thought to change the Sabbath of the Lord, he should select the very day—the first day—to which, above all others, it would be impossible for the Lord himself to change the Sabbath.

We now take our leave of Mr. Elliott and his prize essay; to pursue the subject further would only be to multiply notices of nonsense. In closing, we would simply repeat the remarks already made, that, in consideration of the fact that the Committee of Award decided that this essay was worthy of a prize of five hundred dollars, we should very much like to see an essay on this subject which that committee would decide to be worth nothing. If this essay stands as one of the best arguments for the Sunday-sabbath (and this it certainly does by taking the aforesaid prize, and by its receiving the indorsement of the American Tract Society by a copyright) then the Sunday institution must be in a most sorry plight. And if we had no better reasons for calling the people to the observance of the Sabbath of the Lord—the seventh day—than those that are given in this prize essay for Sunday-keeping, we should actually be ashamed ever to urge anybody to keep it.

As for us, we choose to obey the word of God rather than the word of men. We choose to rest the day in which he has commanded us to rest. We choose to hallow the day which he has hallowed. We choose to *keep* holy the day which he has *made* holy, and which he has commanded all men to keep holy.

Reader, "God did rest the seventh day from all his works." Heb. 4:4. What are *you* going to do? God says, Remember the rest day, to keep it holy. Ex. 20:8. What are you going to do? God says, "The seventh day is the Sabbath [the rest] of the

Lord thy God; *in it thou shalt not do any work.*" Ex. 20:10. What are you going to do?

The word of God is truth. All his commandments are truth. Ps. 119:151. When God has spoken, that word must be accepted as the truth, and all there is then to do is to obey the word as he has spoken it. "It shall be our righteousness if we observe to do all these commandments before the Lord our God as he hath commanded us." Nothing is obedience but to do what the Lord says, *as he says it.* He says, "The seventh day is the Sabbath of the Lord thy God; in it thou shalt not do any work." To disregard the day which God has commanded to be kept, is disobedience. And the disobedience is not in the slightest relieved by the substitution of another day for the one which the Lord has fixed, even though that other day be styled "Christian." The fact is that the seventh day is the Sabbath; and in the fast-hastening Judgment the question will be, Have you kept it? God is now calling out a people who will keep the commandments of God, and the faith of Jesus. Nothing but that will answer. Neither commandment of God nor faith of Jesus ever enjoined the observance of Sunday, the first day of the week. Both commandment of God and faith of Jesus show the everlasting obligation to keep the seventh day, the Sabbath of the Lord thy God. Will you obey God? Will you keep the commandments of God and the faith of Jesus?

APPENDIX.

By special request we insert the whole of Dr. Dobbs's letter, with the one which called it out.

"*To the Reverend Dr. Dobbs*—

"Venerated Man: I rejoice that in you wisdom has its seat, and that you are a sort of plug, so to speak, to which we may, as it were, bring our little pails and dippers to get a supply. Now I am a public speaker, a teacher of morals; in a word, to come right to the point, I am a preacher of the gospel. But I have my troubles; the chief of them is this: I often am compelled to prove something when I haven't got anything to prove it with. What shall I do? how shall I argue without any arguments?

"Pray relieve me, and accept my undying gratitude.

"Yours with remote veneration,
"A Feeble Brother."

REPLY.

"I am happy to say that I have bestowed a good deal of thought on this very point. In fact, here is the very test of real genius. Any person, however frugally divine Providence has dealt by him, can argue if he has anything to argue on; but it takes a master mind to argue on nothing. But it can be done. I have often done it; in fact, 'tis my habitual method.

"Taking the thing to be proved for the proof, is a good way. Thus, it is desired to prove that A is B. You can prove it thus: 'It is universally acknowledged (by all but infidels and radicals) that A is B; hence we see that necessarily A is B, which is the thing that we set out to prove.' Of course, you would not put it just in that bare shape before an audience; I have given you the essence of it; you must dress it up. Thus, you want to prove that the soul is immortal; you prove it thus: 1. The spirit is indestructible. 2. The immaterial part of man is not capable of dissolution; hence, then, we see that the soul is immortal. Properly used, arranged in the flowing robes of ample speech, this is really one of the most effective forms of argument that I know.

"Another, almost equally good, is proving the premise by the conclusion, and then proving the conclusion by the premise, proving A by B, and then proving B by A. And if the people believe the conclusion already (or think they do, which amounts to the same thing), and if you bring in now and then the favorite words and phrases that the people all want to hear, and that they have associated with orthodoxy, 'tis wonderful what a reputation you will get as a logician.

"Proving one thing clearly and conclusively, and then skillfully assuming that you have proved something else, is a master stroke.

"I regard, however, a judicious use of the Fathers as being, on the whole, the best reliance for anyone who is in the situation of my querist. The advantages of the Fathers are twofold: First, they carry a good deal of weight with the masses; and second, you can find whatever you want in the Fathers. I don't believe that any opinion could be advanced so foolish, so manifestly absurd, but that you can find passages to sustain it on the pages of these venerable stagers. And to the common mind, one of these is just as good as another.

"If it happen that the point you want to prove is one that never chanced to occur to the Fathers, why, you can easily show that they would have taken your side if they had only thought of the matter. And if, perchance, there is nothing bearing even remotely or constructively on the point, don't be discouraged; get a good, strong quotation and put the name of the Fathers to it, and utter it with an air of triumph; it will be all just as well; nine-tenths of the people don't stop to ask whether a quotation bears on the matter in hand. Yes, my brother, the Fathers are your stronghold; they are Heaven's best gift to the man who has a cause that can't be sustained in any other way."—*National Baptist*, March 7, 1878.

THE $1,000 PRIZE ESSAY.

"THE LORD'S DAY."

CHAPTER I.

THE INSTITUTION OF THE SABBATH.

SINCE we began the review of the foregoing prize essay, we have received another on the same subject, and with exactly the same design. This too is a prize essay. Not a five-hundred-dollar, but a one-thousand-dollar prize essay. It was written in 1884 by "A. E. Waffle, M. A., [then] Professor of Rhetoric and English Literature in Lewisburg University, Lewisburg, Pa." The prize of one thousand dollars was awarded "after a painstaking and protracted examination," by the Committee of Publication of the American Sunday-school Union; the award was approved by the Board of the Union; and the essay was printed and copyrighted by the Union in 1885. It makes a book of 418 pages, and is printed under the title of "The Lord's Day; Its Universal and Perpetual Obligation."

The author of this book treats the subject in three parts. Part I he devotes to proving the necessity of the Sabbath, by showing that it is necessary to man's physical, his intellectual, his moral and religious, and his social welfare. In Part II he discusses the proposition that "the Sabbath of the Bible was made for all men." In Part III he considers "the nature and importance of the Sabbath." We shall not notice the work in detail because the ground has been mostly covered in our review of "The Abiding Sabbath." About all that we shall do with this book will be to notice the reasons that are given for keeping Sunday, as we want the people to become thoroughly acquainted with the kind of reasoning that draws five-hundred-dollar prizes, and one-thousand-dollar prizes, in proof that Sunday is the Sabbath. We need to make no apology for following up this subject. For certainly a subject to which is devoted so much high-priced discussion, is worthy of notice to any extent to which that discussion may run; more especially when in it there are involved moral and religious principles upon which turn eternal destinies.

The following is a synopsis of chapter 6, Mr. Waffle's argument on the early institution of the Sabbath:—

"Our first argument is founded upon the fact that the Sabbath was instituted at the beginning of human history. . . . In the first three verses of the second chapter of Genesis, we read: 'Thus the heavens and the earth were finished, and all the host of them. And on the seventh day God ended his work which he had made and he rested on the seventh day from all his work which he had made. And God blessed the seventh day, and sanctified it; because that in it he had rested from all his work which God created and made.' . . . The nature of this early Sabbath is hinted at in the words which record its institution. God *rested* from the work of creation. This is evidently meant to teach men that on the seventh day they are to cease from secular toil, and rest. . . . This idea is more fully developed in the statement that God blessed and sanctified the seventh day. . . . Sanctifying the day means that God set it apart as a day to be devoted to holy uses. It could have no higher use than to keep man near to his God and to cultivate his moral and religious nature. . . . It is hardly possible to avoid the conclusion that a Sabbath, on which men rested from secular toil and engaged in the worship of God, was instituted at the beginning of human history. Just as the law of marriage and the law of property are older than the decalogue, so the law of the Sabbath, having its origin in the needs of man and in the benevolence and wisdom of God, was given to the first man, and but repeated and emphasized on Sinai. . . . The bearing of this conclusion upon the general discussion will be readily perceived. If the Sabbath did have this early origin, it was given to the whole race, and should be observed by every human being. . . . The moral law itself is not done away in Christ; no more are the things before it which God made obligatory upon man. Unless it can be shown that the law of the Sabbath, given at the creation, has been repealed by a new legislative act of God, it is still binding upon all men who learn of it. For, coming at this time, it was not given to one man or to one nation, but to the whole human family."

That is the exact truth, well stated. The Sabbath *was* instituted at the beginning of human history. The first three verses of the second chapter of Genesis *are* evidently meant to teach men that *on the seventh day* they are to cease from secular toil, and rest. And it is indeed true that, unless it can be shown that the law of the Sabbath *given at creation*, has been repealed by a new legislative act of God, it is still binding upon all men who learn of it. And that it has not been repealed, that there has been no new legislative act of God, neither by himself, nor by Christ, nor by the apostles, Mr. Waffle shows conclusively. After proving the Sabbath to be a part of the moral law, he advances argument to show that "the law of the Sabbath has never been repealed," from which we shall present a few passages, from chapter 8. He says:—

"If the conclusions of the preceding chapter are just, the law of the Sabbath *can never be abrogated.* So far as it is a moral law it must remain binding upon all men while the world stands. . . . We assert that the law of the Sabbath, so far as it is a moral law, has never been annulled. A law can be repealed only by the same authority that enacted it. It certainly cannot be done away by those who are subject to it. If the law of the Sabbath, *as it appeared in the ten commandments,* has been abolished, it must have been done by some decree of Jehovah. Where have we the record of such a decree? Through what prophet or apostle was it spoken? . . . We can find no words of Christ derogatory to this institution [the Sabbath] as it was originally established, or as it was intended to be observed. All his utterances on the subject were for the purpose of removing misapprehensions or of correcting abuses. It is strange that he should take so much pains to establish the **Sabbath** upon a proper foundation and promote right views of it, if he had any intention of doing away with the institution altogether. . . . The same is true of his actions. There is no record that he ever did anything upon the Sabbath not consistent with its purposes from the beginning. He healed the sick;

but works of mercy on that day were never forbidden except in the rabbinical perversions of the Sabbath.

"It is fair to conclude that Christ never intended to abolish the Sabbath. The only conceivable ground for such a statement is the fact that he opposed the notions of it prevalent in his time. But his efforts to correct these furnish the best evidence that he was desirous of preserving the true Sabbath. He said that it became him to 'fulfill all righteousness.' He voluntarily placed himself under the law, including the law of the Sabbath. Thus he not only maintained the sacredness of the Sabbath by his words, but he also kept it *as an example for us.* . . .

"But do the *apostles* teach that the fourth commandment is no longer in force; that it is not binding upon Christians? It is asserted by many that they do, and appeals are made to their epistles to maintain the assertion. . . . Paul says: 'Wherefore the law is holy, and the commandment holy, and just, and good.' How could he have given it higher praise? And this he says just after the declaration, 'We are delivered from the law.' Does he mean that we are delivered from that which is 'holy, and just, and good,' and that we are henceforth to disregard the things required in the law? Not at all. He simply means that we are freed from the penalty and the bondage of the law. Again he says: 'Do we then make void the law through faith? God forbid; yea, we establish the law.' Here his meaning obviously is that the law is not only honored by the redemption through Christ, but is established in the minds of those who through faith enjoy this redemption, faith giving ability to appreciate its excellence, and power joyfully to obey it. But he is even more specific. When he wants a summary of our duties to our fellowmen, he can do no better than to take the second table of the law. Rom. 13:8–10. . . . Paul was hardly so inconsistent as to quote thus from a law which had been abrogated as a rule of life.

"He is not alone in this practice. St. James says: 'Whosoever shall keep the whole law, and yet offend in one *point*, he is guilty of all. For he that said, Do not commit adultery, said also, Do not kill. Now if thou commit no adultery, yet if thou kill, thou art become a transgressor of the law.' What of it, if the law is annulled? It does not matter if we violate obsolete laws. But James would have said that these laws were still binding, and that no one of them could be violated with impunity. His main point is the integrity of the law—the impossibility of wrenching out one of its members without destroying all. The way in which Paul and James and Peter and John urge upon the Christians to whom they write abstinence from certain specific sins, and the performance of specific duties, shows that those who believe in Christ have need of law. This general view of the relation of Christians to the law will help us to understand what is said by Paul concerning the law of the Sabbath. It is plain that no part of the moral law is abolished. This is still recognized as of binding force upon all. The law of the Sabbath is a part of it, and any apostolic precepts which *appear* hostile to the Sabbath must be interpreted in the light of this fact. . . .

"Our conclusion is that there is nothing in the writings of the apostles which, when fairly interpreted, implies the abrogation of the Sabbath. . . . They honored the moral law as the highest expression of God's will, and say no word to indicate that the law of the Sabbath was not a part of it. Thus both Christ and his inspired apostles have given their sanction to this institution. They have not taken away this choice gift of God to men."

This is sound doctrine. It is true that in speaking of the law of the Sabbath he uses the qualifying phrase, "so far as it is a moral law;" but as the law of the Sabbath is moral to the fullest extent; as there is nothing about it that is not moral, his statement is literally sound. That is, the law of the Sabbath in its widest extent " must remain binding upon all men while the world stands;" and the law of the Sabbath being entirely moral, "has never been annulled." There is more of it that might be quoted, but we have not the space for it. Besides, this is all-sufficient to show the universal and unchangeable obligation of the seventh day as the Sabbath of the Lord.

And now, in view of the fact that the seventh day is the day which God established as the Sabbath at creation; in view of the fact that the seventh day is the day named by God in the fourth commandment; in view of the fact that the law of the Sabbath "as it appeared in the ten commandments," has never been repealed; in view of the fact that Christ kept, "as an example for us," this identical day—the seventh day —named at creation and in the decalogue; in view of the fact that the apostles maintain that "*no part* of the moral law is abolished," and that it is " of binding force upon all ;" in view of the fact that God, and Christ, and his inspired apostles, have given their sanction to this institution, and that in all their words of sanction to the institution there is no reference to anything but the seventh day as the Sabbath; in view of all this, we ourselves would give a thousand dollars, if we had it, to any man who could show, by any process of legitimate reasoning, how Sunday, or any other day but the seventh day, can be the Sabbath.

CHAPTER II.

"THE CHRISTIAN WORLD MUST STAND CONVICTED OF ERROR."

HAVING shown that the Sabbath was given "at the beginning of human history," "for the whole human race, and should be observed by every human being;" having shown that the law of the Sabbath not only has never been abrogated, but that it "*can never be abrogated,*" Mr. Waffle proceeds thus :—

"Accepting the conclusion that the fourth commandment is still in force, it may very properly be asked, 'Why then do not Christians obey it by keeping holy the seventh day of the week, as it directs? By what right is this plain precept disregarded and the first day of the week observed?' This question is a natural one, and unless a satisfactory answer can be given, the Christian world must stand convicted of error."—*P. 184.*

Here are some important acknowledgments. It is acknowledged (1) that the fourth commandment "directs" that "the seventh day of the week" shall be kept holy. This is important in this connection in view of the claim so often made nowadays by Sundaykeepers that the fourth commandment does not refer to any particular day. And (2) it is acknowledged that this "plain precept" is "disregarded" by Christians. We think he does well to state that "unless a satisfactory answer can be given" to the question as to why this is, "the Christian world must stand convicted of error." We are perfectly satisfied that the Christian world must stand convicted of error on this question. And to prove that this is so, we need nothing better than Mr. Waffle's one-thousand-dollar-prize essay; and that is the use that we propose to make of it in this chapter.

The fourth commandment, which Mr. Waffle here admits "directs" that "the seventh day of the week" shall be kept holy, is the law of the Sabbath. Says Mr. Waffle, "The law of the Sabbath can never be abrogated."—*P. 157.* Now as the law of the Sabbath directs that the seventh day of the week shall be kept holy, and as that law can never be abrogated, it is plainly proven that the "Christian world," in disregarding "this plain precept," must stand convicted of error.

Again, Mr. Waffle says:—

"Unless it can be shown that the law of the Sabbath, given at the creation, has been repealed by a new legislative act of God, it is still binding upon all men who learn of it."—*P. 186.*

And:—

"Up to the time of Christ's death no change had been made in the day." "The *authority* must be sought in the words or in the example of the inspired apostles."—*P. 186.*

Then he quotes Matt 16:19, and John 20:23, and says:—

"It is generally understood that these words gave to the apostles supreme authority in legislating for the church. . . . So far as the record shows, they did not, however, give any explicit command enjoining the abandonment of the seventh-day Sabbath, and its observance on the first day of the week."
—*P. 187.*

Now as "the law of the Sabbath" "is still binding upon all men who learn of it" "unless it has been repealed by a new legislative act of God;" as that law "directs" the observance of "the seventh day of the week;" as "up to the time of Christ's death, no change had been made in the day;" as "the authority [for the change] must be sought in the words or in the example of the inspired apostles," to whom (according to Mr. Waffle's claim) was given "supreme authority in legislating for the church;" and as in the exercise of that legislative authority, "they *did not give any explicit command enjoining the abandonment of the seventh-day Sabbath,* and its observance on the first day of the week;" as, therefore, there has been no new legislative act of God—by Mr. Waffle's own words it stands proven to a demonstration that the law of the Sabbath which enjoins the observance of "the seventh day of week" is still binding upon all men, and that in disregarding "this plain precept" "the Christian world must stand convicted of error."

Again we read:—

"If the law of the Sabbath, *as it appeared in the*

ten commandments, has been abolished, it must have been done by some decree of Jehovah. Where have we the record of such a decree? Through what prophet or apostle was it spoken?" "We can find no words of Christ derogatory to this institution as it was originally established, or as it was intended to be observed." "There is nothing in the writings of the apostles which, when fairly interpreted, implies the abrogation of the Sabbath."—*Pp. 160, 165, 183.*

The law of the Sabbath, "*as it appeared in the ten commandments,*" is the fourth commandment. And that commandment, by Mr. Waffle's own interpretation, "directs" that "the seventh day of the week" shall be kept holy. Now as the abolition of that commandment would require some decree of Jehovah; and as no such decree has ever been recorded, nor spoken, neither by prophet nor by apostle, the obligation of the fourth commandment still remains upon all men to keep holy "the seventh day of the week." Therefore, in disregarding this "plain precept," "the Christian world must stand convicted of error."

We must recur to a sentence before quoted. It is this:—

"The *authority* [for the change from the seventh to the first day of the week] must be sought in the words or in the example of the inspired apostles."

Now with that please read this:—

"A law can be repealed only by the same authority that enacted it. It certainly cannot be done away by those who are subject to it."—*P. 160.*

Was the law of the Sabbath enacted by the authority of the words or the example of the inspired apostles? Was it enacted by the authority of inspired men of any class, or at any time? No. The very idea is preposterous. Then it can never be repealed by the authority of inspired men, be they apostles or what not. That law was enacted by the living God in person. And it can never be repealed except by the personal act of the Lord himself. Any attempt of an inspired man to nullify any portion of the moral law *would vitiate his inspiration.* "To the law and to the testimony; if they speak not according to this word, it is because there is no light in them." Isa. 8:20. This is also conveyed in Mr. Waffle's argument: "It certainly cannot be done away by those who are subject to it." The inspired apostles were subject to the law of the Sabbath, as well as to all the rest of the law of God. And to charge to their words or to their example, the change of the Sabbath from the seventh to the first day of the week, is to deny their inspiration, to declare that there is no light in them, and to place them beyond the pale of being men of God. This, too, is even admitted in Mr. Waffle's argument. He says:—

"There is nothing in the example of the apostles to oblige the most tender conscience to abstain from secular employment on the first day of the week, if there is no other authority for observing a weekly Sabbath."—*P. 160.*

Please bear in mind (1) that the aim of this one-thousand-dollar prize essay is to prove that the first day of the week is the true, genuine, and only weekly Sabbath; (2) that the author of the essay admits that the fourth commandment "directs" that "the seventh day of the week" is to be kept holy; (3) and that he likewise declares that the apostles, as supreme legislators for the church, "did not give any explicit command enjoining the abandonment of the seventh-day Sabbath, and its observance on the first day of the week." Then it is plain that all that remains to which he can appeal, and in fact the only thing to which he does appeal as authority for keeping the first day of the week, is the *example* of the apostles. Then when even this he sweeps away with the declaration that "there is nothing in the example of the apostles to oblige the most tender conscience to abstain from secular employment on the first day of the week," his argument leaves not a vestige of authority upon which to rest the observance of the first day of the week. Thus, again, he demonstrates that in disregarding the "plain precept" of the fourth commandment, which "directs" the "keeping holy the seventh day of the week," and which is "still in force," "the Christian world must stand convicted of error."

That is exactly what we have believed for years. It is just what we are constantly endeavoring to set before the "Christian world," as well as before the world in general. And we are thankful that the American Sunday-school Union, by its one-thousand-dollar prize, has enabled us to lay before our readers such a conclusive demonstration of it. We are not prepared to say but what the Union has done a good work in awarding the one-thousand-dollar prize to the essay of Mr. A. E. Waffle, M. A., Professor of Rhetoric and English Literature, etc., etc.; for we cannot see how it would be possible to put together an argument for the first day of the week which could more positively convict the Christian world of error in disregarding the plain precept to keep the seventh day.

CHAPTER III.

SOME ONE-THOUSAND-DOLLAR "REASONS" FOR DISREGARDING THE PLAIN PRECEPT OF JEHOVAH.

WE come now in this one-thousand-dollar-prize essay to the discussion of the change from the seventh to the first day of the week in the observance of the Sabbath. It is true that, as already shown, the author of this essay leaves no room for any change; nevertheless he insists that there has been a change, and insists on giving "reasons" for it. And as reasons to be worth $1,000 ought to be pretty good, we shall, as far as in us lies, give our readers the full benefit of them. To get a full and fair statement of the question before us we shall quote again a passage previously referred to, as follows:—

"Accepting the conclusion that the fourth commandment is still in force, it may very properly be asked, Why then do not Christians obey it by keeping holy the seventh day of the week, as it directs? By what right is this plain precept disregarded and the first day of the week observed? This question is a natural one, and unless a satisfactory answer can be given, the Christian world must stand convicted of error."

Now we are prepared to hear what he proposes

shall be the "satisfactory answer," and which we have good reason to suppose the American Sunday-school Union considers "a satisfactory answer," seeing they paid $1,000 for it. Mr. Waffle's first effort at "a satisfactory answer" is the following :—

"The fact that the observance of the first day of the week is so nearly universal and has been of such long continuance is very significant."

That certainly is not a satisfactory answer. In fact, it is no answer at all. It is simply a begging of the question. But he says it is "very significant." Significant of what? Why, this :—

"It suggests that there must have been some good and sufficient reason for the change."—*P. 184.*

That is to say: The "plain precept" of God has been disregarded by nearly everybody for a long while; therefore there must be some good and sufficient reason for it. In other words: It must be right because nearly everybody does it. But he knows that such doctrine as that will never do, even in a one-thousand-dollar-prize essay, so he immediately adds this caution :—

"Too much should not be made of this, for the church has sanctioned many false doctrines and been tainted by many corrupt practices."

That is the truth. And one of the falsest of her many false doctrines, and one of the most corrupt of her many corrupt practices, is the disregard for the "plain precept" of God as laid down in the fourth commandment, and the substitution for it of the observance of the heathen institution of Sunday, in defense of which Mr. A. E. Waffle writes, and the American Sunday-school Union prints, this essay, which was counted worth a thousand dollars.

His next attempt at a satisfactory answer is this:—

"We have taken the custom of keeping the Sabbath on the first day of the week as we found it; and while this does not exempt us from the duty of inquiry, it throws upon those who question our course 'the burden of proof.'"—*P. 185.*

Can anything be too absurd to find a place in a prize essay on the Sunday-sabbath? Here is a proposition that is contrary to the commonest kind of common sense, as well as to the rules of logic and of evidence. Dr. Carson says: "It is self-evident that in every question *the burden of proof* lies on the side of the affirmative. An affirmation is of no authority without proof. It is as if it had not been affirmed. If I assert a doctrine, I must prove it; for until it is proved it can have no claim to reception. Strictly speaking, it exists only on its proof; and a mere affirmation of it is only an existence on affirmation. If I obstinately refuse proof, I leave my doctrine without foundation, and a simple denial of it is sufficient. No man can be called upon to disprove that which alleges no proof. It is a truth as clear as the light of the sun, that, in every instance, proof lies with the affirmative, or with the holders of the doctrine or rite. If *presumption* has the privilege of casting the burden of proof on the other side, then every man has a right to decline defending his own opinions, and to cast the burden of proof upon those who dispute them. Can anything be more monstrous?" Yet in this grand prize essay this monstrosity is just what is presented as "a satisfactory answer" to the question, "By what right is the plain precept of the fourth commandment disregarded and the first day of the week observed?"

One other statement he makes in this connection, which we wish to transcribe. He says:—

"It is not claimed that the apostles began to keep the Sabbath on the first day of the week immediately after the death of Christ."—*P. 189.*

Then on what day *did* they keep the Sabbath immediately after the death of Christ? Did they keep it on the seventh day, or did they keep no Sabbath at all between the death of Christ and the time when it is claimed they began to keep the first day of the week? In either case, would there not be just as much apostolic example for *not* keeping the first day of the week as there would be for keeping it?

After having begged the question of "a satisfactory answer" through more than five pages, he comes to the discussion of the question of reasons for the change. This he introduces with the question :—

"Was there any reason for such a change?"—*P. 190.*

And in answer to his own question he again begins at once to beg the question thus:—

"If the apostles were guided by the Holy Spirit

when they made it, we need not ask for their reason."

This might be readily enough allowed if the apostles had anywhere told us that they did make the change. But when, as Mr. Waffle himself says, "so far as the record shows, they did not give any explicit command enjoining the abandonment of the seventh-day Sabbath, and its observance on the first day;" and when men insist upon palming off upon us by the authority of the apostles something that the apostles knew nothing about, we insist that we *do* "need to ask for the reason."

But Mr. Waffle continues to beg his question. He says:—

"But since the reality of the change is disputed, we may say that if good reasons for it can be discovered, they furnish presumptive proof that it really took place under divine direction."

But if reasons were discovered which should seem to us good, does it follow that these would be good reasons in the sight of God? Does it follow that these reasons will bear the test of the Judgment? And if, without any command of God, reasons should be discovered which seem to us good for the performance of what we deem religious duties, and we insist upon men's performing these supposed duties, then what is that but to make human reason, instead of the word of God, the standard of human duty? And what is that but to usurp the prerogative of God? And what is that but to imitate the papacy? This is just what is done by Protestants when they insist upon the observance of Sunday, when, even as they admit, so far as the record of God shows, there is no command for it. Though they number to the one hundredth figure their so-called reasons for it, we care not. If there be no command of God for it, there *can be* no reason for it.

At last, by the help of all this beating about, Mr. Waffle actually reaches the place where he introduces the "reasons" which he has begged so hard may be admitted. The first of these is this:—

"One such reason can undoubtedly be found in the abuses which had gathered around the Jewish Sabbath. Christ would not burden his church with such a Sabbath as the rabbis had made; and the easiest way to get rid of these abuses was to change the day."—*P. 190.*

The second reason is:—

"The Gentile churches would never have accepted the Sabbath of the Jews as they had come to observe it."—*Id.*

The third reason is:—

"Christians were not to observe the Sabbath precisely as the Jews had kept it before these abuses arose and while they were acting in accordance with the divine law."—*P. 191.*

To take the space to refute such puerile "reasons" as these, seems to us an imposition upon the good sense and intelligence of our readers. As for the first, if there be any truth at all in it, we should be obliged to believe that Christ changed almost every precept of God; for there was scarcely one which the rabbis, the scribes, and Pharisees had not made void by their traditions and abuses. As for the second, it really has no place; for the great Author of Christianity never asked the Gentile churches, nor any other churches, to accept "the Sabbath *of the Jews* as *they had come to observe it.*" But he does ask all to accept the Sabbath *of the Lord* as *he* himself *observed it*, and as he taught that it should be observed. For this cause he swept away the traditions and abuses that the Jews had heaped upon it. As for the third, what is said there is, in fact, that "Christians were not to observe the Sabbath by acting in accordance with the divine law"(!), which is simply abominable.

But such are the "reasons" for disregarding the plain precept of Jehovah. It was for such "reasons" as this that the American Sunday-school Union, "after a painstaking and protracted examination," paid a prize of $1,000. There is, however, just one redeeming feature of this subject. That is, the author of these "reasons" relieves the apostles of all responsibility for them. He says:—

"We do not say that the apostles saw these reasons and were governed by them. We offer them in explanation of the fact that they were led by the Spirit to make the change, and as suggesting a probability that it would be made."—*P. 192.*

We think Mr. Waffle does well to relieve the apostles from the folly of any knowledge of these preposterous "reasons." And we are certain that all will do well to remain just as far from seeing and being governed by these "reasons" as were the apostles. In this we have an instance of "apostolic example" that we can all safely follow.

Right here we would insert another important consideration. It is this: Why should Mr. Waffle search for reasons, or for any example of the apostles for not keeping the seventh day? He had already written on pages 167-8 of his book (page 137 of this book) that:—

"[Christ] not only maintained the sacredness of the Sabbath by his words, but he also kept it *as an example for us.*"

The only day whose sacredness Christ ever maintained as the Sabbath was the seventh day. The only day which Christ ever kept as the Sabbath, "as an example for us" was the seventh day of the week. Then why does not Mr. Waffle follow that example? Why does he pass by the example of Christ and try to create and hold up before men an "example of the apostles" which differs from the example of Christ? The fact of the matter is, and this point conclusively proves it, that in refusing to keep the seventh day of the week as the Sabbath of the Lord, Christians not only disregard the plain precept of Jehovah, but they also repudiate the example of the Lord Jesus Christ.

CHAPTER IV.

SOME ONE-THOUSAND-DOLLAR REASONS FOR KEEPING THE FIRST DAY OF THE WEEK.

HAVING now seen **Mr. Waffle's**, and the American Sunday-school Union's, presentation of the reasons for disregarding and abandoning the plain precept to observe the seventh day, the Sabbath of the Lord, there yet remains to be noticed the reason why the first day of the week is kept. Mr. Waffle tells us that the apostles "were led to observe the first day of the week as the Sabbath, and gradually to abandon the seventh, by a variety of occurrences which seemed to them to warrant the change, and which, when carefully studied, leave no doubt in our minds that they acted in accordance with the divine intention." But how Mr. Waffle knows that these things seemed to the apostles to warrant the change, he nowhere tells us. And, as the apostles themselves have nowhere said a word on the subject, we have no confidence in Mr. Waffle's imagination of motives which he attributes to them.

Of these "occurrences" he says:—

"The first of them was the resurrection of our Lord. Each of the evangelists mentions very particularly the fact that this took place upon the first day of the week, showing that they felt it important to mark the day. . . . But they might not have given the day the prominence they did if Christ had not distinguished it, by choosing it for most of his appearances to them and other disciples. On the same day on which he arose, he appeared no less than five times. . . . ' But the fact that Christ rose on that day and manifested himself so often to the disciples, *would not necessarily imply a purpose on his part to honor it,* had it not been for *subsequent occurrences.*"—*Pp. 192-194.*

Here it is admitted that our knowledge of the purpose of Christ to honor the first day of the week depends upon occurrences other than his resurrection, and upon occurrences after those of that same day. Therefore, if these "subsequent occurrences" should not be what Mr. Waffle claims, then the fact stands confessed that we have nothing that implies a purpose of Christ to put honor on the first day of the week. Now the first of these subsequent occurrences he relates as follows:—

"For six days he did not appear to them at all, so far as the record shows; but ' on the eighth day, or, as *we* should say, on the seventh day afterwards,' he appeared to the eleven as they were gathered in a closed room."—*P. 194.*

But there is no such record as that he appeared to his disciples "on the eighth day." The reference here is, of course, to John 20: 26, which reads: "And *after* eight days again his disciples were within, and Thomas with them; then came Jesus, the doors being shut, and stood in the midst, and said, Peace be unto you." And when Inspiration has written "*after eight days*," we should like to know by what right, or rule, it is that Mr. Waffle reads "on the eighth day," and then, not satisfied with that, gives it another turn and reads, "as *we* should say on the seventh day afterward." "On what meat doth this our Cæsar feed that he is grown so great" that he can thus boldly manipulate the words of Inspiration? And what can a cause be worth that can be sustained only by resort to such unworthy shifts? It is true that Mr. Waffle quotes the clause from Canon Farrar, but we deny the right of Canon Farrar, or any other man, just as much as we deny the right of Mr. Waffle, to so manipulate the word of God. And it is one of the strongest evidences of the utter weakness of the Sunday cause that, to sustain it, such a consummate scholar as Canon Farrar is obliged to change the plain word of God. But someone may ask: Will not the Greek bear the construction that is thus given to the text? We say, emphatically, No. The words exactly as John wrote them, using English letters in place of Greek letters, are these, "*Kai meth' hemeras okto*," and is, word for word, in English, "*And after days eight*." These are the very words that were penned by the beloved disciple, exactly as he penned them, by the Spirit of God; and when any man, we care not who he may be, changes them so as to make them read "on the eighth day," or "on the seventh day afterward," he is guilty of deliberately changing the word of God, as it was written by his own inspired apostle. And no cause can be the cause of God that is dependent for its support upon a change of the truth of God.

The next occurrence is the claim that Pentecost was on the first day of the week. But even though it were admissible that Pentecost was on Sunday, the word of God is still silent about the first day of the week being thereby set apart and made the Sabbath. And so long as we have only the opinions of men, and these opinions only the fruit of their own wishes, and these wishes supported only by their own imaginations, that Sunday is the Sabbath, or the Lord's day, so long we have the right to deny the truth of it, and to stand upon the "plain precept" of God, which, as Mr. Waffle says, "directs" that "the seventh day of the week" shall be kept holy.

Again Mr. Waffle says:—

"The Christians, at a very early date, were accustomed to hold their religious meetings on that day. The custom seems to have been begun a week from the day of the resurrection (John 20:26), though a single instance of the kind would not make this certain. But there can be no doubt concerning their habit at a later date. We read in Acts, 'Upon the first day of the week, when the disciples came together to break bread, Paul preached unto them.' The plain implication of these words is that it was the *custom* of Christians to meet on that day for the Lord's Supper."—*Pp. 197, 198.*

Notice that he says of this "custom" that "a *single instance* of the kind would not make this certain." Now it is a fact as clear as need be that the instance in John 20:26 was not on the first day of the week. It is likewise a fact that, so far as the word of God tells, the meeting recorded in Acts 20:7 is the only religious meeting ever held on the first day of the week. This, then, being the one single instance of the kind, and as "a single instance of the kind" would not make it certain that it was the custom, therefore it is plainly proved that there is nothing that would make it certain that it was the custom for the apostles to hold meetings on the first day of the week. Well, then, it seems to us that service having for its authority only a custom about which there is nothing certain, is most certainly an unsafe foundation upon which to rest the reason for disregarding the plain precept of Jehovah. Reader, we want something more substantial than that to stand upon when every work shall be brought into the Judgment.

Next Mr. Waffle quotes 1 Cor. 16:2: "Upon the first day of the week let every one of you lay by him in store," etc., and says:—

"It is evident that Paul desires them to bring in their offerings week by week and leave them in the hands of the proper church officers."

It is certainly evident that if that *is* what Paul desires he took the poorest kind of a way to tell it. Just think of it, Paul desires that Christians shall "bring in their offerings week by week and *leave them* in the hands of the proper church officers." And so that his desires may be fulfilled, he tells them, "Upon the first day of the week let every one of you *lay by him* in store." That is, each one is to *lay by him* his offerings, by *leaving them* in the hands of somebody else! And *such* are the reasons for keeping Sunday instead of the Sabbath of the Lord!

There is one more; he says:—

"John speaks of this as 'the Lord's day.' He says, 'I was in the Spirit on the Lord's day.' If he had meant the Sabbath, he would have called it by that name. His expression is analogous to 'the Sabbath of the Lord,' which we find in the Old Testament; but it cannot mean the same day."—*P. 199.*

And why not, pray? "Analogous" means "correspondent; similar; like." Now if the expression "the Lord's day" is *correspondent* to; if it is *similar* to; if it is *like* the expression "the Sabbath of the Lord," then why is it that it cannot mean the same day? Oh, Mr. Waffle's prize essay *says* that it cannot, and isn't that enough? Hardly. Christ said, "The Son of man is Lord even of the Sabbath day." The day of which Christ is Lord, and that day alone, is the Lord's day. But the day of which he was speaking when he said those words is the seventh day. He had not the slightest reference to any other day. He was speaking of the day which the Pharisees regarded as the Sabbath, which everybody knows was the seventh day of the week. Therefore, when "he said unto them," "The Son of man is Lord even of the Sabbath day," it was with sole reference to the seventh day. God had said, "The seventh day is the Sabbath of the Lord," and now when, with sole reference to the seventh day, Christ says, "The Son of man is Lord of the Sabbath," it shows that the seventh day, and that alone, is the Lord's day.

Here we shall present a series of syllogisms on the subject, which will make the point so plain that no person can fail to see it.

FIRST SYLLOGISM.

MAJOR PREMISE: "The Son of man is Lord also of the Sabbath." Mark 2:28.

MINOR PREMISE: "The seventh day is the Sabbath." Ex. 20:10.

CONCLUSION: Therefore, the Son of man is Lord of the seventh day.

Just as surely as the Scripture is true so surely is this conclusion true. Then using this conclusion as a major, we form a

SECOND SYLLOGISM.

MAJOR: The Son of man is Lord of the seventh day.

MINOR: The day of which he is Lord is the Lord's day.

CONCLUSION: Therefore, the seventh day is the Lord's day.

Now with this conclusion as a major, we form our

THIRD SYLLOGISM.

MAJOR: The seventh day is the Lord's day.

MINOR: John says, "I was in the Spirit on the Lord's day." Rev. 1:10.

CONCLUSION: John was in the spirit on the seventh day.

If there is any truth in Scripture or logic, these premises and conclusions are true. Of course the second and third syllogisms are dependent upon the first; but as both the *major* and the *minor* in the first are plain, positive statements of Scripture, the conclusion is strictly according to Scripture. And, we repeat, just as surely as the Scripture is true the conclusion is true, that the Son of man is Lord also of the seventh day; that the seventh day, and that day only, is the Lord's day; and that John "was in the Spirit" on the seventh day, the Sabbath of the Lord. Whosoever therefore would keep the Lord's day must keep the seventh day; for "the Son of man is Lord of the Sabbath," and "the seventh day is the Sabbath."

CHAPTER V.

THE FATHERS AGAIN.

WE verily believe that there never was an extended argument made in favor of the Sunday-sabbath in which appeal for help was not made to the Fathers, and we never expect to see an argument on that subject that does not so do. The treatise now under consideration is by no means an exception. We wish that the American Sunday-school Union, or the trustees of Dartmouth College, or whoever else may have the management of a prize fund, would offer a prize of five hundred or one thousand dollars for an essay on the perpetual obligation of the Sunday-sabbath which should make no mention of the Fathers, and no reference to any human authority, but should be confined strictly to the word of God. Such a production would be worth such a prize as a curiosity in Sunday-sabbath literature, if for nothing else.

To what purpose is a reference to the Fathers anyhow? What is the good of it? Suppose all the Fathers with one voice should say that Sunday is the Lord's day, that the first day of the week is the Christian Sabbath; still to the man who fears God and trembles at his word (and to such alone the Lord looks, Isa. 66 : 2) the question would be, What saith the Scripture? To that question there is but one answer that ever comes to anybody on this subject. That answer is, "The seventh day is the Sabbath of the Lord thy God; in it thou shalt not do any work." The Scripture said to the Fathers, "The seventh day is the Sabbath of the Lord thy God." If the Fathers disregarded it, they sinned, that is all. The Scripture says to the American Sunday-school Union, "The seventh day is the Sabbath of the Lord thy God." If the American Sunday-school Union disregards it, the Union sins, that is all. The Scripture says to Mr. A. E. Waffle, "The seventh day is the Sabbath of the Lord thy God." When Mr. Waffle disregards it, he sins, and when he or any other teaches others to disregard it, he teaches rebellion against the Lord, that is all.

Suppose the Fathers and everybody else from the apostles' day to our own should have disregarded the commandment of God, it would still be just as much our duty to obey that commandment as it would if all had kept it strictly. It is not a question of what the Fathers did, but what they should have done. We are not to interpret the commandment of God by what men have done; but what men have done must be tested by the commandment. The law of God is the immutable standard, and men's actions must conform to that or they are wrong. Mr. Waffle himself admits as much. Thus he says:—

"We are under no obligation to follow the example of Christians who lived in any age subsequent to that of the apostles. *Perversions of Christian doctrine* and *corrupt practices* sprang up so early *and prevailed so widely* as to make such an imitation altogether unsafe."—*P. 203.*

Why then does Mr. Waffle, as well as do Sunday advocates generally, go to an age of "perversions of Christian doctrine," an age of "corrupt practices" so widely prevalent as to make it "altogether unsafe"? This is why :—

"We study their history because it throws *additional light* upon the teaching and the example of the apostles."—*Id.*

Go to an age of darkness to throw additional light upon the age of light itself! Go to an age of "perversion of Christian doctrine" to gain "additional light" upon the perfection of Christian doctrine! Go to an age of "corrupt practices" to gain "additional light" upon the only age of pure practices that the world has ever seen! Study the perversion of Christian doctrine, and the corrupt practices of men, because it throws "additional light" upon the word of God! Use a tallow-dip or a rush-light because it throws "additional light" upon the sun!! To what depths of absurdity will men not run in their attempts to justify their disregard of the commandment of God? What will they not sanction in their endeavors to make void the commandment of God by the traditions of men?

The teaching of the apostles is the word of God, and the word of God is light. Apart from the example of Christ there is no such thing as "the example of the apostles;" and the example of Christ is but the shining of that Light which came into the world, to which men will not come because they love darkness rather than light. And these men, instead of coming to the true Light, run away off to an age of darkness, to an age of confessed "corrupt practices" and "perversions of Christian doctrine," and there, by rummaging around among the Fathers, they manage to find some obscure passages in corrupt texts, and these are seized upon because they "throw additional light" upon the true Light. They run away into the darkness, where all things look alike, and in groping around there they find some men to whom they say, You look like us; you talk as we do; you walk as we do; your views of morals are just like ours;—*you are our Fathers*, and behold what great light is thrown, by your ways, upon the teaching and example of the apostles, *that is*, upon *what we are doing*. True, the apostles said nothing at all about it, but we are doing it, and you did it before us, and that is proof that the apostles intended to do it.

We know that between the Fathers and these their sons there is a most striking family resemblance. They do look alike; they do talk alike; they walk alike; and their ideas of what constitutes obedience to the word of God, are just alike, and we would be fully justified in saying that they all belong to the same family, even though the sons should not own it, but when they take every possible occasion to advertise it and to parade the Fathers as indeed their Fathers, they cannot blame us if we admit it, and do our best to give them the benefit of the relationship. But even though this family resemblance be so perfect that we can hardly tell the Fathers and their children apart, there is one fatal defect about it all, that is, *none of them look like Christ.* Not one of them walks as he walked; for he kept the seventh day, the Sabbath of the Lord. It matters not how much they may resemble one another, the question with us is, Do they resemble Christ? It matters not how closely their words may agree among themselves, the question still is, Do their words agree with the word of God?

We have not the disposition, even though we had the time, to go with Mr. Waffle and the American Sunday-school Union in their one-thousand-dollar excursion into that age where "perversions of Christian doctrine and corrupt practices sprang up so early and prevailed so widely," because Mr. Waffle himself has told us that it is "altogether unsafe," and, besides that we remember a statement in our Guide-Book, written about just such excursions as this, that says: "Be not deceived; evil communications corrupt good manners." Moreover, we have before us the statement of what Mr. Waffle learned by it, and that is enough for us. Here it is:—

"Every statement bearing upon the subject, that can be discovered in the writings of the Fathers, is to the effect that the Christians of the first two centuries were accustomed to keep holy the first day of the week, and that most of them regarded themselves at liberty not to keep the seventh-day Sabbath."—*P. 214.*

The commandment of God, written with his own finger on the tables of stone, says: "Remember the Sabbath day, to keep it holy. . . . The seventh day is the Sabbath of the Lord thy God." But here we are informed that "every statement bearing on the subject, that can be discovered in the writings of the Fathers, is to the effect that the most of them [Christians] regarded themselves at liberty *not to keep* the seventh-day Sabbath." But this is simply to say that they regarded themselves at liberty not to keep the commandment of God. Well, we know a great many people in our own day who regard themselves at liberty to do the same thing; and, like their Fathers, too, they will call themselves "Christians," yea, they will even hold that to be the distinguishing feature of a Christian. The Mormons too regard "themselves at liberty not to keep the seventh-day Sabbath," and also not to keep the commandment that forbids adultery, and they call themselves "saints." Well, if disobedience to that *one* commandment is what makes a Christian, why should not disobedience to *two* commandments make a saint? Will Mr. Waffle or the American Sunday-school Union tell us why?

The commandment of God directs the keeping of the seventh-day Sabbath. The Fathers and Mr. Waffle and other Christians of that kind "regard themselves at liberty not to keep it." The word of God likewise directs the keeping of the commandment which says, "Thou shalt not commit adultery;" the Mormons "regard themselves at liberty not to keep it." The word of God directs the keeping of the second commandment; the Catholics "regard themselves at liberty not to keep it." The word of God directs the keeping of the third commandment; Colonel Ingersoll and his kind "regard themselves at liberty not to keep it." Now upon what principle can these "Christians" convince those "saints," and Catholics, and atheists, of sin? We should like to see Mr. Waffle frame an argument that would show that they are wrong, that would not equally condemn himself, and all those who with him "regard themselves at liberty not to keep the seventh-day Sabbath."

Well, when Mr. Waffle finds that the Fathers, and others of their day, regarded themselves at liberty not to keep the commandment of God, what does he do? Does he say that they were disobedient? Does he repudiate such an example and hold to the commandment of God instead? Not he. He just settles down upon the sinful example as though it were righteousness itself. It is the very thing which he has been all this time striving to reach—something to strengthen and confirm him, and others whom he can reach, in *their* disregard of the commandment. For he says of these writings of the Fathers:—

"Thus they strengthen the conclusion *we have reached* from our examination of the example and teachings of the apostles, that the latter intended to transfer the Sabbath from the seventh to the first day."—*P. 214.*

It never requires a great deal of evidence, nor of a very strong kind, to strengthen a conclusion we have already reached, especially when we have reached the conclusion without evidence. And that such is the way Mr. Waffle has reached his conclusion is plain by his own words. He had already written this:—

"So far as the record shows, they [the apostles] did not give any explicit command enjoining the abandonment of the seventh-day Sabbath and its observance on the first day of the week."

If, then, the apostles gave no command for it, the conclusion which he has reached is, so far as the *teaching* of the apostles goes, totally without evidence. And as he has said that "the authority must be sought in the words or in the *example* of the inspired apostles," when he admits that there is no command for it, he has nothing at all left but what he calls the example of the apostles, upon which to base his conclusion. And upon this we would remind him of his own words, that "the average mind is more readily moved by a direct command than by an *inference* drawn from the *example* of even inspired men."—*P. 242.* He has reached his conclusion, then, by an inference drawn from the example of the apostles. But how does he know and how can he show that his inference is just? Oh, by studying the history of an age of "corrupt practices and perversions of Christian doctrine," he learns "that the most of them regarded themselves at liberty not to keep the seventh-day Sabbath," and that they "*could hardly have made a mistake* concerning the import of their [the apostles'] words and actions." And so having landed himself and his whole Sunday-sabbath scheme squarely upon Catholic ground in the midst of an age of "corrupt practices" and perversions of Christian doctrine, his great one-thousand-dollar task is completed; his grand one-thousand-dollar prize is won, and there we leave him to enjoy it.

We have now examined the reasons for keeping Sunday which have been given in a five-hundred-dollar-prize essay, and in a one-thousand-dollar-prize essay. We have been asked which is the better one of the essays. We can only reply that there is no "better" about it—each is worse than the other. Yet we are not prepared to say that the trustees of Dartmouth College, and the American Sunday-school Union, have done a wholly bad work in paying the prizes by which these essays were put before the world. We are certainly justified in supposing that these essays furnish the very best argument for Sunday-keeping that can be made in the United States; and we think it well that the utter groundlessness of the Sunday institution either in Scripture or reason, should be made to appear, as is done in these essays, even though it be at an expense of $1,500. Yet it does seem a pity to pay so much good money for so many bad arguments, in support of a worthless institution.

The commandment of God reads the same to us that it does to these prize essayists and to everybody else. It says to all: "Remember the Sabbath day, to keep it holy. . . . The seventh day is the Sabbath of the Lord thy God." And for our part we hope we shall never reach the point where we shall regard ourselves at liberty not to keep the commandment of God, for to keep the seventh-day Sabbath is the commandment of God. He who regards himself at liberty not to keep it, regards himself at liberty to commit sin.

TEACH Services, Inc.
P U B L I S H I N G

We invite you to view the complete
selection of titles we publish at:
www.TEACHServices.com

We encourage you to write us
with your thoughts about this,
or any other book we publish at:
info@TEACHServices.com

TEACH Services' titles may be purchased in
bulk quantities for educational, fund-raising,
business, or promotional use.
bulksales@TEACHServices.com

Finally, if you are interested in seeing
your own book in print, please contact us at:
publishing@TEACHServices.com
We are happy to review your manuscript at no charge.

www.ingramcontent.com/pod-product-compliance
Lightning Source LLC
Chambersburg PA
CBHW070539170426
43200CB00011B/2475